Edward Bulwer Lytton

The ring of Amasis

From the papers of a German physician

Edward Bulwer Lytton

The ring of Amasis
From the papers of a German physician

ISBN/EAN: 9783337723729

Printed in Europe, USA, Canada, Australia, Japan

Cover: Foto ©ninafisch / pixelio.de

More available books at **www.hansebooks.com**

THE

RING OF AMASIS.

FROM THE PAPERS OF A GERMAN PHYSICIAN.

BY

ROBERT BULWER LYTTON.

("OWEN MEREDITH.")

NEW YORK:

HARPER & BROTHERS, PUBLISHERS,

FRANKLIN SQUARE.

1863.

CONTENTS.

PART I.

THE DOCTOR.

Polonius. This is too long.
Hamlet. It shall to the barber's with your beard.
Hamlet, Act II., Scene 2.

BOOK I.

The Loreley.

Wherewith she sits on diamond rocks,
Sleeking her soft alluring locks.
MILTON—*Comus.*

BOOK II.

𝔗𝔥𝔢 𝔖𝔢𝔠𝔯𝔢𝔱.

Mac. Canst thou not minister to a mind diseased;
Pluck from the memory a rooted sorrow;
Raze out the written troubles of the brain;
And, with some sweet oblivious antidote,
Cleanse the stuffed bosom of that perilous stuff
That weighs upon the heart?
   Doct.   Therein the patient
Must minister to himself.
   Mac. Throw physic to the dogs. I'll none of it.
                   Macbeth, Act V., Scene 4.

PART II.

THE PATIENT.

To tread a maze that never shall have end,
To burn in sighs and starve in daily tears,
To climb a hill and never to descend,
Giants to kill, and quake at childish fears,
To pine for food, and watch th' Hesperian tree,
To thirst for drink, and nectar still to draw,
To live accurs'd, whom men hold bless'd to be,
And weep those wrongs which never creature saw.

HENRY CONSTABLE.

BOOK I.

A Seed from the Tomb.

The story of my life,
And the particular accidents gone by.

Tempest, Act V.

BOOK II.

𝔗𝔥𝔢 𝔖𝔬𝔴𝔦𝔫𝔤 𝔬𝔣 𝔱𝔥𝔢 𝔖𝔢𝔢𝔡.

Our acts our angels are, or good or ill,
The haunting shadows that walk by us still.

FORD.

BOOK III.

𝔗𝔥𝔢 𝔉𝔯𝔲𝔦𝔱 𝔬𝔣 𝔱𝔥𝔢 𝔖𝔢𝔢𝔡.

In the same hour came forth fingers of a man's hand * * *.
Then the king's countenance was changed, and his thoughts troubled
him.—DANIEL.

CONTENTS.

A 2

INTRODUCTION
BY THE EDITOR.

WHEN my friend Dr. V—— assented (and that very reluctantly) to my reiterated request that he would make known to the public the circumstances herein recorded, I felt myself unable to refuse compliance with the condition affixed by the doctor to this consent, viz., that I should arrange and edit these papers for the press.

I have done so to the best of my ability, and the result is before the reader. For whatever awkwardness or ambiguity there may be in the form of it, the fault is mine. I hope that this confession may induce the doctor's gentle reader not to visit upon him the sins of his editor, but rather to regard him with a greater indulgence.

The strange and somewhat painful confessions which occupy so large a portion of these pages, would appear to have been recorded in the hope that they might contribute at least some hints toward our never-ending research into the moral anatomy of man.

Literature of this kind is perhaps more congenial to the speculative thought of Germany than to the

reading public of England. Still, I am not without a
hope that the doctor's narrative may find among my
countrymen some readers, whose opinion will justify
the present undertaking on the part of his editor.
Thus much in my own behalf. More I will not say,
lest I should appear to be interpreting, without warrant, the intention of a writer who now, in his own
person, claims the privilege of speaking for himself.

OWEN MEREDITH.

PART I.

THE DOCTOR.

Polonius. This is too long.

Hamlet. It shall to the barber's with your beard.

Hamlet, Act II., Scene 2.

BOOK I.

The Loreley.

Wherewith she sits on diamond rocks,
Sleeking her soft alluring locks.

MILTON—*Comus.*

RING OF AMASIS.

CHAPTER I.

THE TUNING OF THE INSTRUMENTS.

THE first of that series of events, under the strong
impression of which I am impelled to write this book,
occurred during the month of July, in the year 1834;
a year memorable, among wine-bibbers at least, for the
excellence of its vintage. As this book is not a biography, and my part in the events I am about to record
is only that of a witness, I am anxious to obtrude my
own personality as little as possible upon the attention of my reader. It will suffice for the present, at
any rate, if he will allow me to introduce myself to
his acquaintance in no more important capacity than
that of a young German doctor, and request him to
accompany me on board the "Loreley" steamer from
Mainz to Köln, whither, on a bright July morning in
the above-mentioned year, I happened to be proceed-
ing on my way to Paris, many reasons, hereafter to
be mentioned, having induced me to seek the French
capital with a view to establishing myself there as a
physician.

Of the small social phenomena of every-day life,

few are more strange than that which takes place on the deck of a passenger steamer.   It is a miracle, and yet a commonplace.   Railway travelers are merely isolated nomads.   Steam-boat travelers, on the contrary, though they may have nothing in common, are nevertheless a community.   Gathered together by the drift of accident from the four corners of the earth—

"Dropped down from heaven or cast up from hell"

—each having suddenly emerged into sight from an utterly impenetrable Past, and soon about to pass out of sight into an equally incalculable Future, it is probable that no two units of this incongruous aggregate ever met before, or will ever meet again; yet here in this particular "confluence of two eternities" they *do* meet, and there is the wonder of it.   They are near neighbors and yet utter strangers.   How curiously, yet how cautiously, does each scrutinize the other, as he inwardly considers the important question, "Do I like the look of him?   Shall I speak to him? or shall it be with us as though he were from Nova Zembla, and I from Timbuctoo?"   All this while, however, the mysterious process of amalgamation is going on, just as surely and methodically as if it were concerned with nothing less than the consolidation of a planetary system, or the development of European civilization from the migration of the races.   The scattered atoms begin to cohere; the chaos to grow into a cosmos; the crowd into a society—a society in which both freedom of discussion and public opinion exist.   National characteristics, too, become distinctly apparent to the studious eye.   Yonder group of stalwart English, pillared in Scotch plaid, and with remarkably windy-looking whiskers, that seem to have contracted in some violent climate a permanent inclination to blow away in opposite directions, are sternly consulting their Murrays, and checking off in a sharp, business-like manner the various "beauties of the Rhine." They look like notaries taking inventory of the effects of a fraudulent bankrupt. My more expansive fel-low-countrymen have already established terms of intimacy with each other. Presently all this will cease. Before nightfall we shall be parceled off to our different destinations; and the lean gentleman in spec-tacles, to whom the fat gentleman in gaiters is just now confiding an interesting family secret, will then only be remembered by his confidential and commu-nicative friend as "a person with whom I traveled from Mainz to Köln."

As soon as I had finally lost sight of the three gray towers of the old cathedral, I seated myself on an un-comfortable green bench near an uncomfortable green table; ordered a glass of punch—stiff, to keep out the morning chill; buttoned my coat across my chest; lighted my cigar, and so pertinaciously followed the bent of my own reflections, that I think I must have been for nearly an hour quite unconscious of the ani-mated conversation which was being carried on with-in my hearing by a little group of travelers who had established themselves by degrees about the bench on which I was seated. Gradually, however, and quite involuntarily, my attention was attracted to their dis-cussion by the frequent repetition of a single word, which created upon me an impression such as I can only convey to the mind of the reader by a digression, for which I hope, on that account, to be pardoned.

Most gentle reader, have you ever listened to the tuning of the instruments in a great orchestra? It has no connection whatever with the overture, yet, in my mind, it is so inseparably associated with the overture, that I confess I miss a certain sense of satisfaction from those concerts to which the musicians enter with their instruments already tuned.

Oh thou dim, mysterious, narrow border-land of the wonderful world of sounds and dreams! Homely old orchestra, dear hast thou ever been to my heart! thou, the single homely, honest thing amid all the gilding and the gewgaws, the flare and glare, of many a splendid theatre!

It is but a meagre strip of dingy space, yet beyond it lies the limitless realm of Faëry. And over that dull-lighted frontier wall, as over a golden causeway bridging the starry splendors, and spanning the infinite spaces, does this poor soul of ours often mount up from all she is, and all she must remain, upon the fretful nether earth, to all she would be, all she trusts to become, in the serene completion of some much-needed world beyond. This is no rhapsody. I feel and believe what I say; and I avow that it is with reluctance, almost with loathing, that I ever look up from the lowly barriers of the orchestra to those sumptuous boxes above it, where the same bloated cherubs eternally leer at each other across the same insipid arabesque. In those boxes sit the victims of the great world's great *ennui*. Fine ladies and gentlemen, who "come late," like Count Isolani in the play; but not like Isolani, who, at least, did not come with empty hands. These come, for the most part, with empty hearts and empty heads. What is Hecuba to them, or they to Hecuba? Far dearer to me, I confess, is that dingy orchestra, behind whose smoky lamps, among whose greasy pulpits, smudged and soiled with the long, long labor of how many an arduous rehearsal, I recognize the great workshop—the strong furnace, wherein the mighty forces of Music toil and toss, and seethe and heave, till, glowing as with strenuous heat, the molten melodies of golden sound flow smooth into the sweet and stately mould of the Master's noble Thought.

How softly, one by one, and with what thoughtful faces, made melancholy by so much loving labor, enter, each to his nightly station behind his dusky music-desk, the gentle makers of sweet sounds! With what tender care the violin is lifted from its little case! Doubtless the poor fiddler's wife has no such showy satin robe as that from which he fondly unfolds his cherished *Cremonese.* It must be an *Amati.* But, soft you! what is that wandering tone, pathetic and yet glad, like the sound of some old fable which we loved to hear when we were children? It is the horn. Thank heaven! the true *Waldhorn*—no new-fangled mechanical cornet-à-pistons. Now the sounds seem straining into unison. You half distinguish faint indications of a coming harmony. Now they fall asunder. All is discord and objurgation. The violin, upon its highest chord, is beginning to confide to the English horn strange news which it has just received under seal of strictest secrecy from the clarionet.

But the bass-viol, with four sharp fifths, breaks in imperative, interrupts the babblers, and severely calls them back to a sense of duty and responsibility. The drowsy double bass, in lazy mood, as he leans against the wall, begins to clear his throat. The lugubrious bassoon gurgles twenty times over his one poor little part, making the most of himself, like an old opera-singer. The trumpet, not having to tune himself, is doing his best to put all his neighbors out of tune. But softly, softly! There sits yonder, by those two brazen bowls, stretched over with dusky parchment, one who seems the master wizard of this wondrous sorcery. His brow is wrinkled into music-scores; his sunken eyes are like two hollow breves; his hair is white and thin. Softly, softly! he taps with muffled wand at the door of the unknown world. And now, sharp through the tuneless tumult, as with a will and a meaning of its own, strikes the shrill, clear, long-drawn, silvery note of the hautboy. Keen-edged and incisive the long note streams, like a sunbeam across the dark, through some chink of a broken wall. And as the dancing motes of golden dust rush into sudden revelation, and begin to waver softly up and down that slant, thin, shining track of light, so now the multitude of foolish notes, smitten by the shrill high note of the hautboy, forthwith enter into the strange significance of that sound, and assume a movement and a meaning not their own.

Reader, this digression is not idle. It closely concerns every incident of this history, throughout which, if you have a musical ear, you who read will recognize again and again, as I who write have been made to recognize it, that particular, unmistakable note of the hautboy. Certainly the conversation to which I am about to refer was to the full as senseless, and far more insipid, than the fitful sounds from my imaginary orchestra; but throughout every phase of it, constantly recurring, dominating all, giving to words insignificant and idle a singular and sinister significance, clear, cold, uncomfortable, premonitory of things to come, I distinctly distinguished that long sharp note of the hautboy.

For years, too, I have been haunted by the sound of it. For years I have heard it, after long intervals of forgetfulness, at moments when I least expected, and was least prepared to hear it. I hear it now as my memory reverts to past events. Perhaps I shall continue to hear it till I have closed this narrative, which, by its restless recurrence, like an unlaid ghost, it has compelled me to commence.

In the present instance it was but a single word that thus impressed me—a word, too, so hackneyed and familiar that I can not account for the strangely unfamiliar sensation with which it affected me.

And what was that word, do you ask?

It was the name of the Loreley.

CHAPTER II.

The Loreley.—Strange Conduct of a Gentleman in Black.

The two small cannons with which, soon after starting, we had saluted the Rheinstein, had long since been charged again, and we were now approaching the spot where they were to enable our little craft to do due honor to her mysterious godmother, the celebrated Loreley. The prospect of so soon passing the abode of that famous enchantress had probably led my fellow-travelers into a discussion of the peculiar character assigned to her by the various legends of which she is the heroine.

A sentimental young lady with a fat waxen face and flat flaxen hair, whose affected accent was of pure Berlin quality, had enthusiastically undertaken (no doubt in the conviction that she was thereby vindicating the cause of sentiment and sensibility) the defense of those anthropophagal tendencies attributed to that melodious Lady Witch, who, to the great detriment of the musical public of former times, is well known to have been in the habit of terminating her concerts by drowning her auditory. This romantic young lady expatiated with so much gusto upon the exquisite poetry and refinement of those very objectionable proceedings on the part of the Loreley, that we all felt persuaded, if she could have sat upon a rock and sung

*Kuken** songs, that the whole of the Prussian army would be forced to take swimming lessons. A slim sub-lieutenant, however, who was there on the way to his garrison at Cologne, appeared to be greatly scandalized by the thought of the disadvantageous and un- . graceful position in which the lords of the creation would be placed when thus compelled to become the ungainly imitators of the four-handed frog. He vehemently objected to the conduct of the Loreley in former times. For his part, he avowed, he had no taste for that antiquated ballad-singer, whose behavior had been simply abominable, and could only have been tolerated under a very imperfect state of the criminal code. Such things were, happily, nowadays quite impossible. He could see in them nothing at all poetical, but much that infringed the police regulations. Any person capable of calmly contemplating the agonies of a drowning man was neither more nor less than a criminal of the worst description, who ought to be—not applauded, but hanged.

Here the conversation was suddenly interrupted by a loud clatter. We all turned round, startled and annoyed. Close to the last speaker, a table, before which had been seated a gentleman dressed in black, and of such unobtrusive appearance that, although every body had seen, nobody had noticed him, was now violently overturned and thrown to the ground. It was impossible to suppose, however, that it had been upset by the stranger, who was at that moment walking away with such profound composure that he did not even appear to have noticed the noise which so much

* A once popular composer of sentimental songs in Germany.

B

disturbed us.   There was, moreover, an indescribable
dignity and grace in the appearance and movement
of this personage, which rendered it perfectly incredible that he should, under any circumstances, be capable of an awkward action.   His countenance was of
that kind which at once compels deference and in-
spires respect.   The bearing and aspect of the whole
man were what you would emphatically distinguish
as unexceptionably *thoroughbred*.   There was nothing
in his features or his manners which repelled, but, on
looking at him, you instinctively felt that it would be
impossible to be familiar with him unless he graciously permitted you to be so.   A vulgar or insolent fellow would not, you felt sure, be able to insult that
man.   As all that is vulgar and mean eludes and escapes the presence of an elevated and select nature so
completely that such a nature can not even take cognizance of the existence of what is ignoble, so I suppose there is in the perfect manners of the great, and
the habitual consciousness of an unapproachably high
social position, something which enables the few who
possess it to pass through the crowd without ever
coming into contact with it.   This man was not only
unapproachable, he was almost invisible.   He was the
image of plastic repose.   Nothing about him was restless, or fidgety, or ill at ease.   It was only by the in-
direct contrast of this extreme tranquillity both in
dress and manner that you unconsciously distinguished him from the ordinary mass of vulgar people
who can not ever sit still or keep themselves quiet.
His features were singularly faultless, but nobody
would have ever thought of calling him a handsome

man. You knew, but you did not notice that beauty of face. His countenance showed neither gayety nor melancholy. It was smooth, and impassive as marble; and, indeed, so inexpressive, that even when you saw him you did not seem to see him; so that, as he now walked away from us, it was only by an effort of memory that we realized the fact of his having so long been present to our sight. Nobody spoke to him, nobody spoke of him, yet every body must have observed him; for when he afterward became the subject of our conversation, there appeared to have been a sort of tacit coincidence and agreement in our previous and separate observations, and we all called him "the Gentleman in Black."

He walked away from the capsized table so quietly and so unconcerned, that one of our party, in perfect astonishment at the inexplicable fall of that awkward piece of furniture, exclaimed to the waiter, who was busily restoring the sprawling thing to its legs, "Holloa! what is the meaning of this? Have you ghosts about here?"

The gentleman who made this inquiry would no doubt have been a believer in table-turning if Mr. Home had emigrated to Europe in the year 1834.

"Well," said another who was sitting beside me, "if it was a ghost, I have seen him, and he was dressed in an infernally well-made suit of clothes, such as none but the devil's tailor knows the cut of."

"Ah!" cried the rest of the party all in a breath; "is it possible? The Gentleman in Black!"

To this explanation of the miracle I strongly objected. It was quite illogical, I asserted, and therefore, to me at least, impossible, to assume that the personage who had just left us was capable of an awkward, not to say an ill-bred act. My ghost-seer, however, assured us all that he had distinctly seen the Gentleman in Black start up suddenly like a wooden figure pushed by a spring, and in so doing upset the table, just as the sub-lieutenant was laying down the law on cases of salvage. As on the strength of this positive testimony I found the majority entirely opposed to my theory of moral evidence, I soon relinquished the discussion and withdrew from the debate.

CHAPTER III.

I DRAW MY OWN CONCLUSIONS ABOUT THE GEN-TLEMAN IN BLACK.

WE were now approaching the Loreley. I saun-
tered to the forepart of the vessel in order to secure a
good view of that famous rock, once so fatal, now so
innocent. As I passed by the funnel, I again noticed
the mysterious stranger about whom we had all been
talking. He was standing alone, close to the little
step-ladder which had just been uncorded from the
bulwarks, and was now slanted forward in readiness
to be let down for any passengers that might be waiting at the next station. He stood erect with folded
arms, and appeared to be contemplating the play of
the violent water as it hissed, and seethed, and bub-
bled about the beating paddle. As I watched that
calm and imperturbable eye fixed upon the boiling
spray beneath, I could not help wondering how the
passions could so completely desert the face of man,
to lavish upon inanimate nature at least the semblance
of intense emotion. The words of the Prussian sub-
lieutenant rushed into my mind. In order to remain
true to his nature, how should this man conduct himself if a fellow-creature were drowning under his eyes?
Would he shout for help? Would he exhort and
stimulate others to the rescue by shaking a purse full
of sequins in their ears like the count in Burger's bal-

lad, *Von Braven Mann?* But how could he do this
without instantaneously abdicating that prerogative
of lofty and unassailable tranquillity which was proclaimed in every feature of his serene and severely
beautiful countenance, in every outline of his self-com-
posed and stately figure? It is told in an old story
that a mortal was once admitted to the assembly of
the gods. He was informed that, of the noble and
majestic forms which he there beheld, one only was a
man; and he was asked if he could recognize his fellow mortal. Amid the true gods, the one man, although he wore golden sandals and a purple fillet, and
drank nectar with the rest of the Olympians, was at
once detected by the *restlessness of his eyes.* Now, as
I silently studied the face of the man before me, I felt
that if one line of those marble features were to change,
the entire expression which commanded my admiration would fall at once like a mere mask, and be detected as a superficial grimace at the mercy of any
rude chance that might choose to pluck it away. The
soul wants not clothes; but if she once puts them on,
they should so finely fit her that she need never take
them off.

Men with such faces as this should never change
countenance, for fear they become contemptible.
"No," I concluded; "that man must remain unmoved by the sight of a drowning creature."

The logic of this conclusion was irresistible, but I
could not reconcile myself to accept it. I was glad
when the cannons were discharged, and the explosion
diverted my attention from the stranger.

The Loreley was not slow to return thanks for this

salute. For my part, I even found her too garrulous. Any little real miracle would have pleased me better than that miraculously natural echo. No subtle song came winding from the wizard rock to enmesh the souls of men in the folly of a fatal bliss. Alas! no such songs are wanted now. The sorcery is fled from the earth; the folly remains.

CHAPTER IV.

UNFORESEEN OCCURRENCE AT SAINT GOAR.—THE
GENTLEMAN IN BLACK DISTINGUISHES HIMSELF.

THE bell sounded from St. Goar. The steamer
slacked speed, and presently a little boat put out from
the land. The only passengers it brought us were a
woman and a child. The woman seemed to be of the
middle class, and the child, a little boy, who was apparently asleep on her lap, might have been about
six years old. Our captain shouted, "Ease her! Stop
her!" from the paddle-box. The paddles stopped
their play, and the vessel drifted leisurely with the
stream. The vast waves that welled up from under
her flanks, as if they were surprised at, and ashamed
of, their own existence in that calm water, dashed off
in a desperate hurry to reach the shore, and there hide
themselves among the rushes. The little boat danced,
and rocked, and dipped among these unnatural undu-
lations.

My thoughts were still coquetting with the Lady
Witch, when I was startled by a sharp and piercing
scream from the water.

"Jesu Maria! my child, my child!"

At the same moment all the passengers rushed in
violent agitation to that side of the vessel where I
was standing by the step-ladder. I at once saw that

the little boat had capsized; but how this had happened I could only guess.

It appeared that the boatman, in attempting to catch the rope from the steamer, had lost his balance, and in the struggle of his fall had brought his clumsy and rickety little craft on her beam-ends. I saw him hauled up the sides of the vessel, while a sailor who had leaped from the ladder succeeded in rescuing the poor woman just at the moment when she was being sucked under the paddle-wheel, and must, but for this timely rescue, have soon perished.

But the child? Where was the child? The steamer had drifted some way down with the current, and we could only see a long way off a small straw hat floating smoothly on the surface of the stream, with its bright blue ribbon fluttering in the wind.

After an instant of intense silence, however, there was a suppressed groan of anxiety from all on board. We could distinctly see the poor little fellow himself struggling desperately, and beating vainly with his tiny hands the headstrong water. His strength seemed to give way. He submerged, and we lost sight of him. No! now there is a loud cry from every soul on board; the little golden head reappears once more above the surface of the stream.

And now, again, there is a deep, agonizing silence. Every eye is strained, every face is sharply stretched in one direction; for in that direction two dark arms of an audacious swimmer can now be seen slowly cutting the waves.

Quite calmly, quite at his ease, with no haste, no precipitation, making each stroke with mathematical precision, as though he were swimming solely for his own pleasure, yet nevertheless with steady strength, as we all can see, leisurely gaining head against the sturdy current, with perfect placidity and undisturbed self-composure, slowly, methodically, onward swims the dark swimmer. I must say there was something almost provoking in the extreme tranquillity, not to say indifference of his movements, upon which we all felt that the life of a human being depended; and the singular and instantaneous accuracy with which the common sentiment of a crowd is always impressed upon the mind of each of its members made me conscious that at that moment the swimmer was an object rather of indignant impatience than of grateful admiration. We all felt that he was not putting forth half the strength which he obviously possessed.

Now, now! he is within but a few arm-lengths of the sinking child. One last effort, one bold stroke, and the poor child is saved! No! Unconcerned, he has let the last desperate chance escape him. One stretch of that strong arm would have done it. One grasp of that firm hand might have easily seized the last patch of the blue blouse which has now sunk from our sight. Too late! The child has disappeared. There is a groan of angry sorrow from the crowd. But it can not reach the swimmer. He too has disappeared from our gaze. My eyes are still fixed upon the spot where we last saw him. There is a silence of intolerable suspense. You can only hear the suppressed breathing of the crowd all round, and the careless sighing of the stream beneath.

That silence seemed as though it would last forever; but after a few moments, which felt like many ages, a loud shout of exultation bursts forth. Far, far away from the spot on which all eyes were fixed — far away he rises again. *They* rise again. "Saved, thank God!" is the universal exclamation.

Now he is swimming back to the steamer more leisurely even than before. He leans upon the current, and lets it quietly bear him along with it. He is lazily pushing his rescued burden before him as if it were a dead thing. He gives it only an occasional impulsion with his hand whenever it seems to interfere with the comfort of his easy and convenient progress. And only an occasional convulsive movement in the limbs of the little body shows that life is not yet extinct. He seems to care nothing for the child he has saved, nothing for the intense interest of which he is himself the object. He appears utterly unconcerned.

And thus the Gentleman in Black regains the steamer.

All this passed rapidly under my eyes. The whole occurrence occupied only a few moments of time — they appeared an eternity. With that keen insight which belongs to strong emotion, I saw clearly into the inmost mind of all those who were around me at that moment. I recognized on every countenance my own agony; I detected in every eye my own thought. In all that crowd there was only one face on which I saw not the reflection of my own feelings; only one eye in which I could discover nothing akin to the sensations either of myself or my fellow-travelers. And suddenly, thrilled as I was by the unutterable regard of that calm, cold, inexplicable eye, I again seemed to hear, with the same uncomfortable sensation, sharp and shrill, from some undistinguishable world of inner sounds, the long-drawn note of the hautboy.

CHAPTER V.

The Loreley in Person.

YES, it was she. Angels and ministers of grace, defend us! She—no dream, but fairer far than all that dreams can fashion—she herself, the Loreley! Beautiful, but with a chill and stony beauty, like the beauty of Medusa, that curdled the blood and froze the veins of men; calm, uncompassionate, pitiless, she was gazing (and I now knew she had long been gazing) upon this death-struggle for life as though the agonies of it were to her the commonest matter of course, and the result of it a subject of supreme indifference. It had been sung to me in songs, I had read it in legends, I had dreamed it in dreams; I could not now mistake that gaze. It was the gaze of the Loreley. She sat as though she had nothing to do but to sleek her beautiful body in the sunshine, while her victims were gurgling their stifled death-cries in the dreadful gulfs far down. She sat, I say, high above the silly crowd; alone, upon the hood of the gangway near which I was standing; isolated, unnoticed, indifferent, even as the Lady Witch upon her rock. Her hidden arms drew tight across her bosom her long silken scarf, which, thus closely draped about her, left distinctly outlined the noble contour of her perfect shoulders. Now that I was suddenly made aware of her presence, I became, at the same moment, instinctively conscious that she had long been there, and that I had all this while been standing within the magic of that strange, cold, beautiful regard, and under the ghostlike gaze of that clear, spiritual eye.   So indifferent to, and so abstracted from the crowd around us —so unlike to, and so dissociate from all others did that strange woman appear, that in now beholding her I at once realized the conviction of how impossible it would have been for me to have noticed her presence until (as in the case of the Gentleman in Black) some accident had forced my consciousness out of the limits of that trivial sphere within which those two apparitions must, I felt persuaded, in obedience to every law of their nature, remain invisible.

A new boat had now been sent out from the steamer, and the child, apparently lifeless, was picked up and brought back to its mother.   The strong swimmer, by whose exertions the little boy had been recovered, refused all assistance from the boat, and swam slowly after it toward the steamer.   Nobody any longer paid the least attention to his proceedings.   And while the crowd on deck gathered with noisy but heartfelt congratulation round the poor mother, the savior of her child entered the vessel unperceived.

I myself had not noticed his return.   I remained spellbound and immovable under the melancholy eye of the Loreley; and I was still absorbed in the intense contemplation of the perplexing passionlessness of that Gorgonian face, when I suddenly perceived that he was standing before her.

But how changed were his features!   Now, for the first time, I fully recognized all the noble beauty of them; for now those features were animated, for the first time since I had seen them, by an expression, and that expression was one of mute but passionate prayer. The whole countenance worked and labored with the concentrated action of internal forces. The painful quivering of the lip, the deep imploring of the earnest eye, all were agonizingly eloquent with the pathos of that unuttered appeal. And calmly, coldly, upon that imploring face, from the lofty heights of her chilly self-isolation, the beautiful Loreley looked down in silence, with the cruel dead tranquillity of her empty, unanswering, extinguished eye. Then, as with a supreme effort, from the long-laboring lip of the man before her, a voice, broken and hollow, inarticulately muttered these words—"*Still never?*"

And sharp, freezing, and incisive as the long shrill note of the hautboy was the answer of the Loreley— "*Never!*" It sounded—(that short stern word, that meant so much, mocking the word it answered)—like a ghostly echo in a hollow, empty ruin, where nothing but such an echo any longer dwells.

For a moment the face of the man was swathed in a livid pallor as of death. The next moment those marble features had completely resumed their habitual repose, and he disappeared down the staircase into the cabin, noiseless, calmly, almost imperceptibly, as when, some hours before, I had seen him leave the table just as it clattered down at my feet, and so greatly startled us all.

At that moment I was called away to attend to the child, and thus lost sight of the Loreley. This was my first actual practice as a physician. A glance at

my little patient sufficed to assure me that only very
simple restoratives were needed. And, having spoken
a few words of encouragement and reassurance to the
mother of the lad, I was turning away to give the necessary directions to the steward, when a gray-headed
valet-de-chambre, the perfection of neat decorum, presented himself before us, and, bowing to the poor woman with that deference which is only manifested by
the servants of persons of the highest breeding to
those whom they assume to be of lower rank than
their masters, respectfully requested the good woman,
in the name of the Count and Countess R——, to do
the count and countess the favor to join them in the
private cabin, and to bring with her the little boy, for
whose comfort and refreshment every preparation had
been made.

Thus I finally lost sight of the four human beings
who were in any way associated in my mind with the
mysterious side of that day's events; and, once more
on the deck of the "Loreley" steamer, the great Commonplace resumed "her ancient," but not "solitary
reign."

CHAPTER VI.

PUBLIC OPINION.—WE REACH COLOGNE.—THE OLD CRANE ON THE OLD TOWER, AND WHAT IT SEEMS TO BE SAYING.

PUBLIC opinion on board the "Loreley" steamer was much excited by the recent occurrence. Every body was asking, "Who is the Gentleman in Black?" The steward, who was naturally our chief source of information on this subject, could tell us nothing more than that the name of the strange gentleman, whose conduct had excited such conflicting feelings and inspired so much curiosity among my fellow-travelers, was Count Edmond R——; that he was the possessor of an immense *majorat* in Prussian Silesia, and the last descendant of a well-known and very ancient family.

The mysterious Loreley thus receded from the luminous realms of Fable, and only revealed herself to the common light of day as a Silesian countess! The stern and terrible sorceress, by whose spells I had been so magically mastered, was, by indisputable evidence, neither more nor less than the wife of Count Edmond R——. Others, however, besides myself, had noticed the extraordinary, and more than human indifference which had characterized the conduct of the Witch, now reduced to the rank assigned to her by the *Almanac de Gotha.* She too, the wife of so noble a husband! a man of whom any woman (so we all averred) might well be proud! How had it been possible for that woman to watch with an eye so callous, and a countenance of such avowed and heartless unconcern, the noble conduct of the count, when, at the imminent risk of his life, he swam to the rescue of the drowning child? As you may well conceive, all the women vehemently condemned the countess, and loudly extolled the count.

In particular, the sentimental young lady of the waxen-flaxen charms, who that morning had so warmly defended the cause of the imaginary Loreley, and elaborately extolled the poetry and sublimity of the various misdeeds attributed to that duly-patented and well-established witch, was now emphatic, not to say hysterical, in the expression of her indignation at the heartless affectation of the countess.

I may mention by the way that this young lady, at the moment of the recent catastrophe, had been duly careful not to let slip so favorable and appropriate an occasion for a little shrieking and fainting, which, on the whole, had been tolerably successful. The Prussian sub-lieutenant, for his part, declared that the count had shown great incompetence, and was quite undeserving of the ignorant applause which had been lavished upon his supposed skill and coolness. He assured us that, but for the respect he paid to his uniform, and if he had not had straps to his trowsers— (for indeed he might say, for the first time in his life, he had positively envied the gentleman on the Civil List)—he would have shown us all the proper way of saving a drowning person. That the child had been actually saved was, he assured us, entirely due to the merest chance in the world; or rather, indeed, if the truth must be told, to his own perspicuity and energy, since he it was that had given express orders to send a boat to the swimmer, whereby the child had been taken up, though out of vanity, as every body could see, the count had refused for himself the proffered assistance. In all such cases it was absolutely necessary to follow a quite different method from that which had been adopted in the present instance. It was a mercy that the result had not been fatal. He had himself studied the true principles of natation at the Schwimm-Schule at Potsdam. For the practice of these principles, however, it was necessary to have a special costume properly adapted for the purpose.

These views were opposed by a merchant from Hamburg, who observed that the chief danger to be apprehended in all attempts to rescue a drowning person exists in the frantic efforts made by the drowning man to save himself, or in the involuntary cramps and convulsions which, so long as consciousness lasts, not unfrequently impede the efforts of the rescuing hand, and are known to have often proved fatal to both parties. The merit of the count was in the calm and composure which he had had the presence of mind to preserve. Every body could see that he might have hastened his speed, and that it would have been easy for him to have reached the child before it sank. But he rightly waited till the little limbs were exhausted; and so accurately calculated his distance, that the body must have reached him under the water in an exact line with the point at which he dived to secure it. This explanation was received as so satisfactory, that the Prussian sub-lieutenant, twisting his mustaches, growled out something about *Bürger Philister*, and stalked away with a loud clanking of spurs and sabre.

The countess, however, was not without her defenders among the men, who, on the strength of the opinion offered by the Hamburg merchant, readily adopted the assumption that the count was no doubt so admirable and experienced a swimmer that his wife need have been under no reasonable apprehension for his safety.

At this point in the discussion, one of my fellow-travelers, who till then had not joined in the conversation, informed us that some years ago he had had occasion to visit Heligoland, and that he had there heard the name of Count R—— frequently mentioned as that of a most intrepid and unrivaled swimmer. The feats attributed to the count by the fishermen along that coast appeared indeed almost incredible. One of his exploits in particular was much talked of at the time.

One dark and tempestuous night a fishing-boat was wrecked within sight of land, and the alarm was given along the coast that all souls on board were in imminent danger. The boldest fisherman, however, did not dare to brave the breakers that night, and no man could be found who was willing in such a storm to expose his life to the hazard of an enterprise so absolutely desperate. Suddenly a mysterious stranger appeared among the terrified crowd. He said nothing, he betrayed no emotion, but every body seemed to feel the presence of a superior will, and silently made way for him. He quietly picked up five of the great cables which had been hopelessly flung by in the conviction of the impossibility of attempting a rescue. With the same composure and undisturbed precision, he firmly bound together with a small cord the ends of the five ropes, and, taking the cord in his left hand, he silently plunged into the sea. In this way he succeeded in saving the five souls that were on board the sinking craft. That stranger was Count Edmond R——. And as, by a sort of instantaneous tacit instinct, we had all of us this morning given to the mysterious count the somewhat sinister title of "*the Gentleman in Black*," so the poor fisherfolk of Heligoland, ever after the event of that night, distinguished the heroic stranger by the more grateful appellation of "*Newfoundland*."

Hence, no doubt, the indifference evinced by the countess on the present occasion.

We all very cheerfully accepted this explanation of the lady's conduct, till, to our no small astonishment, a certain very portly Königlich-Preussischer-Wirklicher-Geheimer-Ober-Bau-Rath declared that the whole of Silesia knew perfectly well that the countess was touched in her mind.

This mental affection, he presumed, must be incurable, as he had never heard that any sort of treatment had been tried for it. The Count and Countess R—— lived in extreme seclusion all the year round at the count's *majorat* about ten miles from Breslau. They saw nobody; nobody ever saw them. There was no direct heir to the estate, which would lapse, at the

death of the count, to the collateral branch; and,
therefore, nobody in Silesia was at all concerned about
their affairs.

This strange and unlooked-for announcement silenced all farther conversation upon the subject. The
little group of talkers soon afterward broke up and
dispersed, for we were approaching the end of our
journey, and every body except myself seemed satisfied to dismiss the matter from their minds.

What were precisely my own feelings as I walked
musingly back to the bows of the boat, and leaned
over the yellowing waters, it would be hard to say.

Deep under the death-white shroud of a profound
and settled melancholy, which seemed to have permanently swathed in its cold and colorless beauty
the faultless features of the countess, my heart had
detected the buried presence of an unutterable sorrow.
One moment of luminous agony had revealed to me
in the dark eye of the count the torture of a soul
surely smitten by no earthly hand. "No," I said to
myself. "Of the secret of these two souls, whatever
that may be, I have at least seen enough to feel sure
that it involves them both in the anguish of an *irreconcilable destiny.*"

The accident of the day now nearly closed had so
long delayed the course of our little steamer, that the
sunset was far spent when we passed slowly under the
darkening walls of the old imperial city of Cologne.
The evening was hushed and sleepy. Dreamlike we
seemed to glide into the shadow of the ancient town.
Above the deep and drowsy orange light that was
now burning low down in the wasting west, rose, dark

and calm into the airy twilight of the upper sky, the
massive tower of the huge Cathedral. And high upon
the summit of that tall, dark tower—high, and still,
and solitary, as some old wizard on the watch, stood
the giant crane, which is ever the first object to greet
the eye of the traveler who enters Cologne.

Lonely and aloof under the darkening sky it stood,
with its long, gaunt arm stretched out, as though in
wild appeal, toward the antique Dragon-stone, from
whose venerable quarries had been hewn, age after
age, and block by block, the vast pile on which it now
stood—companionless between earth and heaven. To
scale to the height of that supreme solitude had the
heart of the Dragon rock been broken, and year by
year his mighty limbs in massy morsels wrenched
away; and now, alone under the melancholy stars,
pillared upon piles of pillage, there stood the hoary
robber, gazing sadly, as it seemed to me, at the wrong-
ed and ruined rock. As I lifted my eyes to that solitary image, so lifelike and so lonesome, with ever outstretched arm, and long-appealing gesture, seeming to
look eternally in one direction, as though listening for
an answer which will never come, I fancied that the
old crane might be saying to the old rock, "Irrevocable is the Past, and sad and weary is the coming and
the going of the endless years. And now, of the ancient time, are we two left alone upon the earth. Let
us be reconciled to each other."

BOOK II.

The Secret.

Mac. Canst thou not minister to a mind diseased;
Pluck from the memory a rooted sorrow;
Raze out the written troubles of the brain;
And, with some sweet oblivious antidote,
Cleanse the stuffed bosom of that perilous stuff
That weighs upon the heart?
    Doct.   Therein the patient
Must minister to himself.
    Mac. Throw physic to the dogs. I'll none of it.
                        Macbeth, Act V., Scene 4.

C

BOOK II.

CHAPTER I.

Biographical and Parenthetical, containing sundry Reflections upon the Relative Position of Physician and Patient.

As events are to be told *quorum pars fui*, it seems fitting that here, if any where, I should say something about myself. On this subject I have not much to say.

It was a justifiable custom of the old masters to paint their own portraits in the foreground of their pictures; nay, even to represent themselves therein as saints and apostles. Saints and apostles they were in their pictures, if not out of them, and this no matter how well their tavern-doings may have been known to the pious public of their day.

But I have no such pretensions. Few men have hands strong or steady enough to hold up the mirror to their own nature, even in private. But to do this in public demands a courage which, happily, I am not called to evince, since I am writing only of others, *non tam sagax observator, quam simplex recitator.*

I lost my father when I was three years old. Perhaps the waters of the Beresina still roll over his unburied bones. My only knowledge of him was gathered from my mother's talk, and a miniature which represents him as a young cavalry captain in a French regiment.

In the year 1806 he was quartered with his garrison at B——, in Thuringia, where he made the acquaintance of my mother's family, and asked her hand in marriage — a stranger, a Frenchman, an enemy! You may conceive that my father's offer was civilly declined by the family. Still, the charm of my mother's beauty and goodness was such that he could not reconcile himself to this refusal. In 1808 he was at Erfurt with the Emperor; obtained a short *congé;* revisited my mother's family; and so agreeably impressed them all by the cordiality of his manners, and the sincerity of his affection for my mother, that they could no longer refuse their consent, and the marriage was hastily concluded.

My mother accompanied her husband to France, where I was born, at St. Cloud, in 1809.

In 1812 my father's profession again called him to arms. On leaving my mother, he promised her that this campaign should be his last. He kept his word. Amid the snows of the Beresina he perished.

My mother returned with the child to her own relations, and settled in Germany. She never married again, but devoted her widowhood to my education.

The first face to which my eyes were accustomed was a sad one. My mother's grief endeared to me the thought of a father whom I had never known. The story of his early death, and of the sufferings of those who perished amid the frozen steppes in that disastrous retreat of the French army from Russia, I was soon familiar with. These stories made a profound impression upon my childish mind, to which I trace the passionate longing that impelled me, from my earliest years, to embrace a profession of which the object is to mitigate suffering and combat disease. This was my hobby even in the days when I was only able *equitare in arundine longo* — to ride a-cockhorse on a stick.

The face of my father on the miniature haunted my imagination in childhood. I seemed to see him perishing, neglected, upon the frozen banks of the Beresina; his dying eye turned on me, and his hand outstretched in vain appeal for help. I persuaded myself that his life might have been saved by the medical care and assistance which in those hideous solitudes it must have been impossible to obtain. My eyes ran over with tears; and when my mother said, "What is the matter with the child?" I flung myself into her arms and said, "Dear mother, when I am a man, let me be a physician."

My mother was the only one of her family who encouraged in me this desire, which strengthened as I grew up. Her relations were scandalized to think that the member of a noble family should voluntarily become the member of a profession noble only in the beneficence of it. However, my own strong resolution, and my mother's gentle firmness, carried the point. A physician I became, and a physician I am; so far, at least, as the certificates of professors, some experience, and an ardent love of science can make me.

In the Faubourg St. Germain were still living some

of my father's relations. This fact, but yet more the advanced state of medical science in France, decided me to begin my career as a physician in that country. I was on my way thither on the occasion that made me a witness to the events recorded in the preceding chapters.

Between me and those events there was now a space of two years, and between me and the Rhine the mountain chain of Les Vosges.

About this time I resolved to quit my modest chambers on the *Quai St. Michel.* There, for two years, a very spider of science, I had hung my dingy web over the roofs of the most renowned hospitals in Europe, and dwelt, *tanquam in speculo positus,* ever ready to pounce upon each "interesting case," as the unsentimental language of medicine designates the most excruciated victims in the great torture-chamber of Disease. My time during these two years had not been wasted. I might now, if I pleased, return home with no meanly stored experience of the infinite domain of medical science. But I could not make up my mind to quit the most luxurious and refined capital in the world without having devoted some time and attention to what is called Society, in proportion as it is socially exclusive.

Some of my father's family still occupied high positions, and were able to introduce me to those spheres of the Paris world which, ever since the days of the Grande Monarque, have monopolized, almost without interruption, the despotic government of European taste and *bon ton.*

Know, therefore, oh most dear and much revered

Reader, that my address until farther notice is, *Rue, et l'hôtel, de la Paix, au premier,* wherein, moreover, *nota qua sedes fuerint,* replacing cases numberless of specimen bones, gleam cabinets of buhl and porcelain vases. In lieu of lancets and Latin memoranda, invitations, Opera-tickets, and *billets-doux* strew my table and stuff my looking-glass. The hardly-earned title of "Doctor in Medicine" has disappeared from my visiting cards, and is replaced by a title due only to the accident of birth. I rise late, with the sun of Fashion. I lounge over the dainty breakfast of a delicate dandy. The lightest of phaetons or the neatest of English hacks takes me to the Champs Elysées and the Bois, or else I saunter on the Boulevard arm in arm with some one of the myriad friends—so lightly won, so lightly lost—wherewith that pleasant pavement is besprinkled ever. A dinner in the bow window at the Café de Paris, a stall at the Opera, and three or four *soirées* in the Faubourg, finish my day of strenuous inertness.

Whereat you shake your honored heads, oh my much disapproving, much respected friends!

Yet grant me a moment of your patience. I am *nunquam minus otiosus quam quum otiosus.* In pleading my own cause, let me vindicate that of a profession dear to my heart.

The doctor!

Dreary, living memorial, maintained by the sighs of humanity in homage to the Fall of Man!

Doctors, undertakers, and hangmen are beings whose presence society only puts up with because it can not do without them. Nobody wishes to see

much of them. Doctors! pah! ghouls! who remind
us that we are nothing but a network of veins, mus-
cles, and nervous fibre! Cynics of the dissecting-
room, whose eyes are sold to the contemplation of
sickening things, whose minds are made up in the
mould of a harsh materialism! Doctors! nightmares
of mankind, which endures them with a groan only
because each man, as an antidote to prejudice, carries
in him a strong dose of superstition, and believes,
when his body begins to plague him, that his dear life
is in the hands of the leech.

So the doctor is a despot after all, and rules by the
fear of death. But society revenges itself. Despotism against despotism.

Let the doctor dare only so much as lift his eyes, in
the hope and love of a man's heart, on the daughter
of the noble house whose life he has just snatched
from the opening grave with an energy and a skill
unknown perhaps to science without love, and frigid-
ly you ask for his bill, and sublimely you ring the
bell, and honestly you feel that rather to the arms of
Death than to the arms of a doctor would you confide
the rescued treasure.

I have much considered this.

In exaggeration itself the true measure can be found,
since there it must be, otherwise how should it be ex-
ceeded?

Something of error I find on either side.

"There must be division of classes and distinction
between ranks," says the World. The World says
well. He is a fool that would gainsay it; and whoever fights against Prejudice must expect to be worst-

ed; for the odds are all to one. However hard this
may appear, it is just.

I have seen in how cruel a dilemma those unhappy
ones are placed who, yielding to an impulse not otherwise than noble, have outraged the prejudice of
class, and overleaped the barriers which it raised between two hearts. In the lives thus violently united
I have detected an irremediable schism. And even
there, where shame and pride suppressed the groan
of conscious failure, to my eyes, accustomed to trace
them, a thousand symptoms have revealed the presence of the hidden worm, whose morose tooth, made
more intolerable by the necessity of concealing the
wound on which it worked, was gnawing disappoint-
ed hearts.

True, I have also examined cases wherein all the
world's exactest requirements had been obediently
fulfilled, ay, even to the precise satisfaction of its highest pretension—cases of failure wherein, nevertheless,
rank, name, fortune, age, bodily and mental advant-
ages, all reciprocities in short, were in unison to a degree that might sustain the quantitative analysis of
Lavoisier. The temple was accurately built, but within the walls of it no divinity abode.

Of all cases, these are the most puzzling.

One easily understands that disobedience to a law
should entail unhappiness, if by obedience to the same
law happiness is secured.

The Law of God, for instance, is entitled by all laws
of logic to avenge the infraction of it. For fools may
murmur as they will, but let any man loyally obey
that law, and I will defy him to be unhappy.

C 2

But where this is not the case, where the strictest obedience to the law does not, as a necessary consequence, insure that happiness which disobedience forfeits, surely there must be "something rotten in the state of Denmark."

Let us not fear to say it: 'tis the law itself that is rotten.

In what? Perhaps in this:

Cease to be *personages* only, and become *men*, if you will not forego the prerogatives of man. Cease to live by convention in the narrow pride of position, and begin to live naturally in the large pride of humanity, if you would enforce Nature's warrant to search life for human joy. But take heed—do not deceive yourselves. If you are conscious that Nature is not in you, that *men* you are not and never can become, then in God's name stick to your ranks and conventions, and thank Heaven that these, at least, enable you to be *something*.*

All things are easier to us than to become fully and integrally that which we originally and naturally *are*. And if the dog-philosopher who, two thousand years ago, went about in the world with lantern lighted at midday to look for a *man*, were now again among us, perhaps he would no longer be at the pains even to

---

* Had my friend ever read the poems of Charles Churchill, he might have found in the following verses something like an anticipation of this thought:

"'Twas Nature's first intent,
Before their rank became their punishment,
They should have pass'd for men, nor blushed to prize
The blessing she bestow'd," etc.

CHURCHILL—*Independence.*

search at all, but would blow out his lantern and keep contentedly kenneled in his tub.

"Vix sunt homines hoc nomine digni."

But Diogenes was a cur. The noble mastiff is not to be roused by the snarling of a mongrel. To nothing less than man's sympathy for man can man's worth reveal itself.

Between Christianity and Socialism there is all the difference in the world. Christianity says to the rich, Give. Socialism says to the poor, Take. A notable distinction! Let us seek, not to equalize, but to har-. monize ranks and classes.

" And who is better qualified to do this," I said to myself, "than the Physician—he whose subject and whose object are man ?"

To find man in the Patient by showing to the pa-tient man in the Physician—this was my purpose.

Patient and Physician. Do not these represent the two most salient sides of humanity?

The sufferer: deserving love, because most needing love.

The healer, the restorer: deserving love, because most competent to love.

After all (may the ghost of Galen forgive me for saying it!), Medicine, if it be a science, is the science of guess-work and divination. The physician's business is to guess what Nature needs. All that books can teach is to him no more than the flight of the birds, or the hue of the entrails to the augur—mere aids to intuition. Sympathy is the sole source of div-ination, for only sympathy can interpret the unknown. Sympathy is revelation.

Love one another, and help one another. You may write a thousand volumes upon ethics, but you will not add a jot to the divinity of this doctrine.

Well, this was the road that led me from the Quai St. Michel to the Rue de la Paix.

I say there are faults on both sides.

My duty thenceforth was to combat mutual prejudice.

The faults of the Physician, as a class, I knew. To emancipate myself from these needed only a strong will and strict adherence to a few simple principles deduced from personal experience. But from the faults of other classes to emancipate the patient? Of this I knew nothing, and felt that I never should know any thing so long as I suffered myself to see in my patients nothing more than so many scientific "*subjects.*" Certain ills there are which are only consequent to the manners and customs of a class.

How should the Physician cure these?

Submit to a medical regimen the many ways of living of the many classes of society?

You can not do it.

Prevent young countesses from going to balls, prevent old gentlemen from drinking too much generous wine at sumptuous tables, prevent young gentlemen from passing their nights in playing at cards and drinking Champagne, by all means. If you can do this, Napoleon, by the side of you, was a tyro in the art of government.

But if the enemy is not to be banished by this or any other means, then let us study more narrowly his mode of warfare, that at least we may diminish his force and resist his attacks.

The inferior classes are easy of access. They invite the approach of the observer.

The doors of poverty are off their hinges, and hang open.

Roofless and naked, misery crawls at your feet.

The middle class opens its hand to you with a welcome, and spontaneously lays bare to your friendly eye the process of its daily life. To this class the educated physician brings with him a fragrance of refinement which pleasantly refreshes an atmosphere close and clogged with the taint of the till and the store-house. In the middle class the family doctor is the family friend.

Utilize to the utmost the advantage of your position, oh my brothers in the healing art. You are the friends of mankind at large, for the foe you contend with is all men's enemy, therefore you stand in singular relation to all classes. Mediate between them. The Divine Physician of humanity was content to call himself a Mediator. Mediate, also, ye. Three times an hour you are called from the straw pallet to the princely couch, from the pauper's hovel to the rich man's mansion. Here as there, in this as in that, pain meets your eye and claims your care; for Disease, like Death, beats with equal foot on the thresholds of the rich and poor, and to you man's weakness opens the doors which are shut by his pride. Every where you have seen the equality of suffering. Every where you may mediate the equality of happiness.

But the doors of the great are guarded by an army of lackeys. In the houses of the great it is only the sick-room that opens to the physician. When the fear of death passes the door of that room, it strikes down the barrier which convalescence makes haste to rebuild.   And if from time to time you meet again in the great world the woman who, in her hour of supreme anxiety, flung out wild hands, and wailed to you for rescue, she will henceforth be to you only an apparition in which the arts of the toilet and the lessons of the dancing-master are combined to deceive your penetration, and lend to the body of disease the graceful semblance of a charm whose substantial virtue is only in the gift of health.

In that smiling vision of a pretty woman, bosomed in an airy cloud of palpitating gauze, with brows whereon the diamond lights defiance, and eyes that sparkle with the triumph of an hour, what shows you the cankerous thing that is gnawing at the core of the vital coil—gnawing at the core so fast, that haply from that brilliant apparition of the ballroom to the wretched image on the bed of death there is but a fainting-fit, a syncope, a moment's giddy change?

I do protest it amazes me to have seen men whose names it is the pride of science to record—men who, to the patient gasping in the agony of death, have predicted the day and hour of his recovery—stamp their feet with angry impatience as they were leaving the door of some fine lady's boudoir, where, on costly cushions of the softest silk, the delicate *migraine* had spread its dainty couch.

Oh ye Samsons of science, whose strong hands have broken the jaws of young lions, and beat the baffled fever from his dearly-rescued prey, witless as babies worried by a gnat have I seen you, unable quite, for all your pains, to stop the small, small noxious humming of that infinitesimal insect commonly called *nerves!* Have I not heard you loudly denying its existence in the very moment when you were bullied, baffled, beaten by the exasperating buzz of it? And then do you abuse the poor patient for not being able to emancipate herself from a morbid imagination. Emancipate *herself?* as if to be the emancipator were not specially *your* business, and this morbid imagination the very disease it behooves you to deal with!

"Don't drink strong tea; don't jade your nerves in crowded rooms; don't tire your strength in the night-long dance!"

Is that all you have to say to the sufferer?

But they do drink strong tea; they do go to crowded balls; they do dance from morning to night. They do nothing else, indeed.

Well, and what then?

Ether and sal volatile, and you are at the end of your pharmacopœia.

Bah!

Sympathizing reader, do you now understand what induced me to seize the favoring chance that offered me admission into favored circles? My object there was two-fold. I wished to rid myself by friction with the brilliant surface of that world of the angularities of professional pedantry which the physician acquires from the habits of the dissecting-room and the hospital ward, where he must harden his susceptibilities against the piteous moan and supplicating look, in order that his steady eye may miss no movement of the hand of the professor who is sawing the hipbone or sewing the femoral artery of No. 73, and then hurry on to No. 87, without pausing by the bed where they have just thrown the death-sheet over No. 78.

I also wished to acquire and appropriate to my own uses those fine tones and delicate touches of exterior culture which are the art of the higher classes; for let it be fully acknowledged, the Great are artists; artists of the beautiful in common things, artists in the preservation of the graces of daily life. I am thankful to think that in human nature the tendency toward nobility is so ineradicable, that while, on the one hand, vulgarity itself is but a clumsy homage to something above, on the other hand, even there, where nature is most artificial, Beauty receives its ultimate tribute in the perfected amenities of intercourse and purified forms of expression. For this, I faithfully respect those who, as a class, are faithful to the respect of themselves. Greatness is made up of little things greatly treated; and it is no small thing to realize in little matters the large sense of that lofty motto, "*Noblesse oblige.*"

With the result of my attempts to analyze the subtle perfume of that brilliant flower called High Life, in order that in the same corolla which contained the dainty poison I might find the delicate antidote, I have no reason to be dissatisfied. I acquired, indeed—less by any scientific skill than by that tact which is the gift of daily experience—a reputation greater than my deserts.

But throughout this chronicle of fates not mine, I am resolved to speak no more about myself than what absolutely concerns my relation to the life of others.

I am writing, as it were, under a spell; and the ghosts that have set this task upon me are already impatient, as I think; for again I seem to sit before the half-up-lifted curtain of the drama of a dream; and again, as long ago, from far away into the hearing of my mind is borne, in warning or in menace, the phantom haut-boy's melancholy note. By the side of thee, my Read-er, I sit down, glad of thy safe human presence here, confronted as I am by these ghostly memories.

And now of thee also gladly-would I know as much as of me thou now knowest, oh my Reader.

CHAPTER II.

APPARITIONS.

IN this daily round of trivial circumstance my pleasantest hours were when, alone in the Bois de Boulogne, I let the reins lie idly on my horse's neck, and lazily indulged my own inclinations in suffering him to follow his. I speak of the old Bois de Boulogne, the Bois of many years ago, whose quiet groves were dear to solitude; not the new-made forest of to-day, which is chiefly dear to Fashion and the *Demimonde*. Not more pleasant to my horse's feet was the soft, thick-shaded sand along the thousand leafy alleys where he led me at his will and pleasure, than to my heart those many pastoral haunts so near to Paris, so far from the world, along the wooded banks of the Seine—smiling Surène, or Mon Calvaire veiled in soberest autumn air. But chiefly I loved, and oftenest sought, that part of the wood where, as you ride, at intervals behind the warm bird-haunted brakes you see in the pure, clear evening light the gleaming of the quiet Mare d'Auteuil.

There, in true German fashion, I used to dream away the yellow ends of many an idle afternoon. For there, a weeping willow hangs over the glassy water, yearning to some mirrored image which it well knows how to hide. There the tall Italian poplars stand a-tiptoe, high above the comely trunks of good old oaks

contentedly half hidden in the mazy thicket underneath. But to those poplars comes the evening breeze
with latest tidings of their own fair land. That is
why they are so pensive all day long. The water itself feeds there, with constant cool, under the heavy
summer heats, the green roots of a paradise of blooms.
The iris, with his yellow cloven helm and sharp two-
edged sword, steps boldly forward from the blossomy
brinks. Like a little tree out of the crystal pool, up-
shoots, with graceful pyramid of white, thick-clustered
flowers, the delicate alisma. Midway along the liquid
dark float all day long at ease the large leaf-isles of
the nymphæa. And there the restless water-spider
weaves his swift-dissolving wizard circles round the
dreamy, half-closed calyx of the lotus, leaning low.

Thither one evening, from the little village hard by
where I put up my horse, I had strolled in time to see
the setting sun of October twinkle through the airy
webwork of the half dismantled grove. I was sitting
upon the roots of a hollow tree, and gazing at the
west, where, though the sun was sunk, dark, bright-
lipped clouds were dipping their moist mouths into a
lingering liquid fire, to breathe it back in sombre light
upon the shadowed land.

"Here," I said to myself, "so near the noisy metropolis of the world, is the very perfection of solitude!"

At that moment, across the profound calm of nature, I heard a voice of pain crying "Cain! Cain!"

There was something in the suddenness and the
sound of that voice which made me shudder.

Startled, I looked all around me. I could see no

human being.   Every bird was silent in its nest.
And still the voice cried "Cain!"

Then silence.

From the grated greenery of the willow-tree not far
off the voice had issued.   But I sat still, stupefied and
bewildered, without courage to approach that spot.

Again in accents of intensest pain the voice began
to speak.   Listening with a creepy awe, I heard it cry,

"If thou wilt destroy me, dreadful Hand—if thou
art sworn to sink me to the abyss—why then dost
thou not pluck me by the hair, or seize me by the
throat, and drag me down into the deeps from which
thou risest thus?   If thou wilt have my heart, why
dost thou not pierce this long-tormented breast with
but a single sharply-daggered ray of thine intolerable
amethyst?   Be any thing but what thou art.   Rise
rather on my path—not thus, cold Hand, not thus—
but with fist firm-clenched, and arm of weightiest
menace.   Then will I grapple with thee hand to hand,
ay, even till my bones be broken in thine iron grasp.
But stretch not forth thus piteously to me those pale
imploring fingers.   Not thus!   I can not seize thee
thus, thou knowest it well; for fast the devilish amethyst has fixed me with his demon eye, and it burns,
it burns—away!"

Then from the twilight shadows of the glimmering
willow a man came forth, and instantly disappeared
elsewhere into the dark and lonely woodland.

Instantly, yet not so soon but what I had recognized his face.   I had never forgotten that face.   The
man I had just seen was the man I had seen two years
before upon the deck of the "Loreley."

It was the Gentleman in Black.

I was strangely agitated by the unexpected and momentary reappearance of this man.

Night had long fallen, and all was dark around me before I could rouse myself from the stupor of amazement into which I had been cast, no less by the mysterious and unintelligible words which I had overheard, than by the vivid recollections and undefined curiosity which those words had conjured back to my mind.

But at length I was conscious of a chilly change in the night air. I got up and walked back with bewildering sensations to the little village where I had left my horse.

My head was already in a whirl when I mounted and rode homeward. I rode fast, feeling that I was late, but hardly knowing how or where I rode.

A strong wind had risen, and violently swept forward, up the road, twirling columns of fine white sand. I could see them plainly; for it was one of those nights in which the sky is darker than the earth, and the land was covered with a gray, melancholy glare. They moved sometimes beside me like spectres as I galloped on, or

"Lapland giants trotting by our side;"

sometimes they rose erect before me, and paused and hovered on the road as if in menace. To watch them whirling and changing shape as I galloped through them made me giddy. I felt my brain getting troubled, and my sight confused.

Suddenly, on the summit of a tall, dark tree (as it

seemed to me), I saw solemnly seated a strange, pale figure. It, too, I recognized at once. It was the figure of the woman I had seen two years before seated in the same attitude on the hatchway of the steamer. It was she herself, the Loreley!

Her dark mantle had slid from her cold white shoulder—cold and white as marble. Her long hair beat the wind. And a high, wild song of jubilee and lamentation—a song of deepest joy and deepest sorrow, she was chanting or wailing in the plaintive murmur of the midnight storm. A song of subtlest sorcery it was; unearthly sweet, and wild with more than mortal pain; in meshes of a music magical bewildering every headlong sense, and leading blindfold to the brinks of death the soul it thrilled with solemn shuddering and a deep delight. I felt the madness growing in me as I gazed with charmed and spellbound eyes upon the melancholy face of that alluring apparition.

While I was yet looking at it, unconscious of all else, my horse shied, and sprang aside with a frightened bound. I lost my stirrup. The reins fell from my loose hand. Confused and afraid of falling, I tried to throw my arms round the neck of the horse.

Suddenly, as in a dream, I perceived that all the place was changed, and the things about me other than they were. The forest had disappeared, and given place all round to bare, black, pointed rocks, whose sharp peaks grazed with rugged edges the sullen sky. About the base of these black rocks fierce breakers, roaring, dashed their foamy surge, and tossed in air white mists of chilly spray.

That to which my arms were clinging fast was not my horse's neck, but the prow of a broken, sinking bark. That which I had taken for columns of white dust was a tumultuous crowd of desperate swimmers, shipwrecked like myself.

And we fiercely jostled each other, and fought and pushed, and struggled all together in the roaring gulf.

But high over all this, alone under the starless, dark night-sky, aloof upon her reachless rock, sat cold the Loreley. And her calm intolerable eye was fixed upon that writhing knot of hideous human faces.

There, in the violent waters, all human passions seemed let loose—Desire and jealousy, and love and rage, and rapture and despair; and in every stormy face the waves were tossing up and down, the passions of man contended more fiercely than the elements of nature in revolt. Each desperate swimmer was fiercely struggling to the savage rock where sat the Loreley. Each frenzied eye that glittered from the seething surge was fixed with hopeless passion on the face of the Sorceress.

And still she sat, and still she sang her solemn song, the cruel fair Enchantress!

But as, one by one, each fierce, impassioned face was singled sharply out from the heaving human mass, and struck by the intense look of that cold eye that watched them from the rock, the face thus paralyzed fell back, still staring to the last with glassy looks upon the Loreley, and dropped into the waves and disappeared. Each maddened swimmer, as that eye fell on him, flung up his arms, and was whirled away upon the roaring gulf, and seen no more.

And still she sat, and still she sang her solemn song; and still we helpless swimmers beat the boiling billows, and still the drowning men strove fiercely till they sunk.

At last I, too, felt myself suddenly touched by an icy ray from the eye of the Loreley.

Then toward her I stretched forth my arms, and cried,

"Oh Loreley! dear Loreley! and I, too, suffer. But I believe in thee, dear Loreley. I do not think that thou desirest my destruction, though in thee I feel my fate. Speak to me, speak to me, oh fair and far away, and tell me, tell me, that thou art she whom I have ever loved and must love evermore! Hear me, dear Loreley! speak to me, Loreley! say to me, say to me, 'Yes, I am she—I am Song; for I am the voice of your hearts, ye forlorn ones. But out of your hearts I am fled—long since, far away, and forever; for in them I could not abide. Forever, forever I have left ye, and ye seek me—forever, forever. And empty ye wander, and tuneless. Weary ye stray in the desert, and sad with your orphaned souls. And ever the poor soul is wringing her hands, and in vain. And ever she yearns, and ever she calls *Come back! Come back!* to the voice she remembers, and pines for, and mourns—the voice of your hearts that is fled. And ever without rest ye are urged to recapture that winged voice which from far, far off, makes moan.

"'But never that voice shall return to you; never, never shall you hear it save in the accents of an eternal longing eternally unfulfilled. Never shall the querulous chord that vibrates to the music of that voice find resolution; never shall the panging of your spirits be at rest. But in your pride ye perish. For never patient of the impossible, ever ye strive, and ever strive in vain, to overpass the bound that separates from your desire at its height, the height of a satisfaction which you contemplate in pain. And in the supreme moment of your desperate endeavor, when with wild hands and clamorous hearts you clamber at the summit, then with broken limbs you are hurled backward, and subside into the abyss.' . . . Tell me this, dear Loreley. Tell me that it is not thou who dost destroy us. And if I must never attain to thee, ever at least let me love thee, oh thou fair and far away !"

I cried I know not what, but words like these of passionate appeal. And tears, hot tears, were falling fast from those deep eyes, no longer cold or callous, of the Loreley.

They fell like soothing dews into the boiling, vaporous surge, and made sweet stillness on the violent waves. Then in that stillness, tenderest sounds of unimagined sweetness sunk softly down, and bathed with blissful music all my throbbing brow.

"Yes," the sweet sounds answered, "it is I. Thou hast known me. Thou hast divined my song. And the heavy curse which banished me, and bound me to the barren rock, is fallen away, and I come to thee, poor soul ! I come."   •

Lower, lower from her lonely place, and nearer, nearer to me leaned the Loreley. Her white hand hovered over me in the hollow dark.

My own right hand in ecstasy I stretched, and seized   *   *   *   *   *

D

CHAPTER III.

AND WHAT THEY LEAVE BEHIND THEM.

THIS was all I could recollect when, many days afterward, I began slowly to recover from the effects of the violent shock I had received in falling from my horse.

A *fiacre*, returning empty from Auteuil to Paris on the evening referred to in the previous chapter, had found me lying senseless on the road. I must have fallen with violence against the trunk of a tree, for I had a severe contused wound on the forehead. And I suppose, from the torn state of my clothes, that in falling I may have caught my foot in the stirrup, and been dragged by my horse some yards along the road; for my hands were badly cut, and my coat completely in tatters. My visiting-cards, and the address on one or two letters which he found in my pocket-book, had enabled the cabman who picked me up to bring me to my own house, where I remained insensible for many days.

The fantastic details, therefore, which, by an effort of memory, I have carefully put together in the preceding chapter, must have been only the images rapidly painted on the receding skirt of a dream (the hallucination of a giddy brain in a moment of delirium) by a consciousness already confused between fact and fancy. And the whole of my imaginary adventure with the Loreley, on which memory, in the mind's waking state, had impressed those proportions which are inherent to the habitual sense of time and space, must in reality have occupied only a few seconds.

I was convinced of this by a fact which enabled me to recall, with an accuracy that would otherwise, perhaps, have been impossible, the circumstances which preceded and those which accompanied my fall, and which proved that up to the moment when I first saw the apparition of the Loreley I was in full possession of my senses.

On the evening when I was brought home senseless by the driver of the *fiacre*, my valet, in trying to get my clothes off me, found my right hand so firmly clenched together that he had to force open the fingers. He then perceived that the hand was closed upon what it had doubtless been grasping when it was stiffened by the sort of tetanus produced by the violence of my fall—a piece of crumpled paper. As this paper was covered with writing which he could not understand, the valet surmised that it might possibly be of some importance, and, instead of destroying it, he put it aside, and placed it in my hands when I was sufficiently reccovered, with the explanation here given.

I unfolded the paper carelessly enough, and glanced at it with indifference, convinced that it could contain nothing of the least interest; probably a prescription, or some old medical memoranda of no use to any body; and I was just about to toss it aside with a sick man's usual impatience, when my eye was caught, and my interest instantly aroused, by these words written

in German: "Fatal Hand, forbear! forbear! Why so
heavily bruise a heart already broken?"

"This," I exclaimed, "can be no mere chance;" and
with an ardor as great as my previous indifference, I
began to read the manuscript. The characters were
pale, and in many places quite effaced. The paper itself was so torn that the fragment was often quite unintelligible. I pieced the writing out, and put it together with extreme difficulty. So far as I could succeed in making any thing out of it, it ran thus:

"*   *   *   [ch?]ase me, with never any
rest, from land to land? Fatal Hand, forbear! forbear! Why so heavily bruise a heart already brok-
en? Finish thy hateful work. I offer thee my throat.
Throttle me, once for all, with those stiff fingers. I
lay bare to thee my breast. Crush it! crush it in
thy giant grasp! Stifle here for evermore the painful breath of life; in its own cradle let it find its
grave. And thou! thou whom   *   *   *   *
more than a brother! Why must it needs have been
thou, thou of all others who   *   *   *   *
*   the fatal ring   *   *   *   wicked
chance   *   *   *   into thy hand? Had I
not staked on it all my heart's felicity? all my soul's
salvation? Did I not see in that moment the amethyst which Hell   *   *   *   *   *   in-
fernal flaming of those fires   *   *   *   *
even then, when   *   *   *   *   imploring
me   *   *   *   *   *   *   jealous demon   *   *   *   *   too late!   *   *
*   *   Every where under the water   *   *

* * in vain! in vain! * * * *
* brought senseless home? Then speech died on
my lips. Then in search of death I wandered over
the world. Was I not ever foremost in the ranks of
those who were vowed to destruction by the wrath of
the savage Tscherkess? Like the Roman of old who
had heard, to his hurt, the voice of the augur, wrapped
in the robe of despair, blindfold I rushed into the
heart of the battle, invoking the gods to devote me
'to the dead and to Mother Earth.' In vain! in vain!
With a sigh of relief I saw the sword flash bare above
me; with a sigh of relief I watched the muzzle of the
gun leveled at my head by the eye that never errs.
What balked them of a willing victim? What turned them from their certain aim, and my release?

"Ever, ever the same! on the rocks of the Caucasus; amid the camps of the Circassian; in the howling Baltic billows; in the battle and the storm; that
Hand! Why did I start like a stricken man, and
fall to earth, when unawares I saw it on the stretched
forefinger of a common sign-post glittering at me?
Then when, by my fall (thy work!) we were all saved
from imminent sudden death under the tumbling
rock? Ever thy ghostly hand, fearful protecting
spectre! Enough! my punishment is greater than I
can bear. What right hast thou to rob the grave?
Let me die. * * * * * Felix! Felix! * * * * that should have blessed
me, that has been my curse! And when the priest
* * * * * * our union, did I not
see in hers * * * * * * that
froze the marrow of my bones? * * She

herself, had she not seen it sparkle? And then   *
*   *   *   *   *   *   *   *   the frightful secret suppressed for years with the force of a
giant, and endured with the fortitude of a martyr   *
*   *   *   *   *   *   in a moment of
mad delirium! Ay, from the lips of fever the burning breath of hell streamed into her heart, and seared
all pity in it, and hardened it forever!   *   *   *
*   *   forever!   *   *   *   *   *   *
I saw her in the silent morning light, when all the
world was still and holy—I saw her when, in the
stillness, my heart was lifted up. Then when I began to bless God, thinking 'surely the bitterness of
death is passed,' I saw her by my bedside, watching
—another spectre!   *   *   *   *   *   and
her eyes were on me, and I could not answer her
question."

Here the fragment ended. I could have no doubt
that the writer of it was Count R——, and that, in
some way or other, it had passed from his hands into
mine. I had distinctly identified him with the solitary figure I had seen issuing from the willow-tree
immediately after I had overheard those strange words
which had so strongly affected my imagination, and
between which and the contents of this page of manuscript I could now trace an obvious connection. The
count may have been not far from me, somewhere in
the forest at the time of my fall. This paper, which
looked like the page of a private journal, he may have

had with him at the time. Perhaps the wind had swept it away, perhaps he himself may have torn it out, crumpled it up, and tossed it from him, not deeming that the darkness of that night could have any eyes to read it. This paper, fluttering on the wind, and gleaming white in the night air, may have been the very thing which frightened my horse; the very thing which I had seized in my giddy trance, as I fell, supposing it to be the hand of the Loreley.

The events recorded in the first part of this book, and which I witnessed on my way to Paris, had made upon me an impression hardly to be accounted for by the nature of the events themselves, which had in it nothing at all extraordinary. I had seen a boat upset, and a little boy rescued from drowning by a Silesian nobleman, who appeared to be a practiced swimmer, the husband of a woman of great beauty, with whom he did not seem to be very happily united. There was nothing wonderful in all this. Little boats will upset if they are carelessly managed; men who know how to swim will do what they can to save little boys from being drowned; and beautiful women will live on bad terms with their husbands, without any special exertions on the part of Fate.

But there are moments in life when, without any apparent preparation, some unseen Power lifts aside the veil which hides from our inward eye a world of things obscurely apprehended.

In the dead stagnant flats of daily life, when we have only a sleepy sense of being, and the leaden weight of accumulated triviality weighs us down, and keeps us low and lazy in the muddy bottom-bed of

the running river of life, we are easily satisfied, because our desires also are low and muddy—

"Rising to no fancy flies;"

and we perceive not then the spiritual breeze that
lightly ruffles the surface of the living element.   But
sometimes the deeps are disturbed, or sometimes we
must come to the surface for air, and then we behold
in a moment of time a world of strange, new things,
bright, and sharp, and vivid, as they *really* are, and
not flat, and faint, and hueless, as the smeared image
of them is imperfectly reflected on the dull and heavy
ooze of our customary perceptions.

There are undoubtedly moments of preternatural
vision when the whole mind is in the eye, and achieves
for our knowledge of the universe in man what the
telescope achieves for our knowledge of the universe
outside.   It annihilates time and space by calling the
invisible into sight and bringing near what is distant.
Lovers sometimes have this faculty of vision in moments of passion; poets in moments of genius.   The
former, in such moments, know each other's hearts at
a glance; the latter, in such moments, know the whole
world's heart at a glance.

Shakspeare, one might almost think, must have been
in permanent possession of such a gift.   When he,
whose intuition seems superhuman, undertook to de-
pict the birth of love, it is noteworthy that he did not
select for the expression of it a single word from the
inexhaustible treasures of his vast vocabulary.

In the thick of a thoughtless crowd two human beings meet each other.   These two beings exchange a

single momentary look, and all is consummated. Nothing has been said, and all is said. Nothing has been done, and all is done. The chain of Fate snaps fast both ends of it, and shuts before, behind. Every link in that chain of fatality is the logical sequence of a necessary law. We call it Love. And for the highest *earthly* expression of it, we know no other name than Romeo and Juliet.

It is worthy of notice how lovers are never tired of talking about eternity. With them every thing, however common, assumes colossal proportions. They are to be satisfied with nothing less than Forever. The vulgarest of men, who is probably incapable of loving any thing for more than a few hours, does not scruple during those few hours to exercise a lover's established prerogative, and prate of eternity as though it were his to dispose of. Blame him not. He is sincere. What is the reason of this?

It is not hard to find. For what is Eternity but that which, being present, absorbs into its own presence, and so fully possesses, both past and future? Lovers do this when they love, even though their love may last but a moment. That moment *is* eternity. All that it contains belongs to eternity, and stands in vast and superlative proportions to the mean relations of time.

But such moments of intuition are not exclusively the property of lovers and men of genius.

It was in such a moment, years ago, on the deck of the "Loreley," that (I know not how) the entire fate of two hearts had been laid bare to my eye at a glance; and that so clearly, that I seemed to feel through and through their feelings, and look through and through their eyes, into the deepest depth of their being, without needing the knowledge of a single circumstance in their lives to guide me through the labyrinth of their lot. It was clear to me in that moment that what these two beings possessed in common was that which must eternally divide them from each other— a thought irreconcilable to union. I can find no other expression for what I mean; for what I mean is only vaguely expressed to my own apprehension.

But I was powerfully affected by what I saw and what I felt in that moment, and I am aware that it has impressed a special direction upon all my subsequent turn of thought and course of study.

From that moment all my studies were to me only in the sense of so many levers wherewith I was in hopes to force from its sockets the shut door behind which are the mysterious chambers of the mind. It appeared to me that we doctors ought to bring all our endeavors to culminate on that point of being wherein the two-fold nature of man both falls together and falls asunder. It is not the body only, nor the mind only, which we have to consider as a thing by itself. Vainly we satiate fever with quinine if we can not simultaneously provide the needful opiate for a worried brain; and vainly shall we administer morals to a mind diseased if we can not give support and energy to the will by healing ministrations to the body. Hence the necessity of investigating the conditions of alliance between the different dynamics of life. *Alterius sic altera poscit opem.*

Extraordinary!

With this interjection we are apt to dismiss from our minds those subjects to which we grudge even the most ordinary attention.

"Very remarkable," say we, thereby meaning that which 'twere waste of time either to mark or remark.

Yet it is by extraordinary revelations that ordinary facts become explicable. Mad-houses and their inmates (not always perhaps so pitiable as in our world of sober sadness we esteem them) received my frequent visits. I followed with attention even the ravings of fever, but was specially studious of my own sensations.

Such studies, I confess, must necessarily remain imperfect, because therein the mind is simultaneously the subject and the instrument. To this I trace the comparatively small result hitherto attained by metaphysics.

I made my servant wake me frequently during the night, that I might, as it were, seize in the act the furtive process of my dreams, compare the influence of different hours, different conditions of body, and record my impressions while they were yet vivid.

These observations were destined to form materials for a psychological treatise, the completion of which I reserved for maturer years.

Thus, I had little difficulty in anatomizing my recent hallucination in the Bois de Boulogne.

The events of more than two years ago, on board the steamer, had filled the background of my brain with a series of indistinct images or ideas. My second unexpected encounter with the count had, by a sudden shock to the imaginative faculty, forced these im-

ages into the foreground of Fancy, thus approaching
them nearer to reality.   Realities themselves had simultaneously, in the tumult of the elements, assumed a
fantastic character, thus approaching nearer to the action of the imagination.

The whole vision, with all its retinue of sights and
sounds, had doubtless occupied but a few seconds in
its passage over a brain already bewildered by the
rush of blood, in which consciousness was at last extinguished.   When I opened my note-book to record
this new experience, I found that my last entry was as
follows.

CHAPTER IV.

Theory of Apparitions.

" Die Geisterwelt ist nicht verschlossen ;
Dein Sinn ist zu, dein Herz ist todt."

"Unlocked the world of spirits lies ;
Thy sense is shut, thy heart is dead."

GOETHE—*Faust.*

SPECTRAL apparitions? phantoms? ghosts? visions?

Pooh! effects of imagination! nonsense!

Granted: for us, who do not experience them; but for the ghost-seer, the visionary, what is proved by the fact that what *he* sees *I* do *not* see?

The verdict of the senses, negative to me, is affirmative to him; and if the thing imagined have no real existence, the imagination of it is not the less a reality. The proof of the *apparition* is that it *appears.*

What we call The Evidence of the Senses will, I think, if analyzed, be found to consist of two distinct activities—Sensation and Inference.

Sensation alone can not constitute the act of intelligent perception—such, at least, as for all practical purposes we regard it.

For instance, we do not *see* the solidity of any object; we *infer* it. We do not *see* the cause of any sound; we *infer* it. Nay, we unconsciously infer the *images* of all objects from the nature of the action excited by the objects upon the nerves of sensation; for, though the images of objects are reflected upon the retina, they can not be reflected upon the brain; nor are they even reflected upon the retina in the position which is given to them by intelligent perception. Sight, therefore, is not an *image*, but a *sensation*. The *image* exists only in the *thought* produced by the sensation.

Hence intelligent perception depends upon accuracy of inference rather than acuteness of sensation, and accuracy of inference must depend upon experience. It is so strong a tendency in our nature to project consciousness, as it were, by referring all sensation to external objects, that, if the act of inference (which completes what, for want of a better term, I must be content to call intelligent perception) were not constantly subordinated to judgment and experience, we should be led to ignore, or, at any rate, to misapprehend that vast range of subjective sensations which constitutes so large a part of our consciousness.

There can be no doubt, however, that we are capable of seeing, and that very clearly, objects which have no immediate external counterpart, and hearing sounds, as well as tasting flavors, and smelling odors, which have no external cause. For instance, after looking at any object in a bright light, we shall continue, long after we have ceased to contemplate it, to see the same object depicted in various colors upon a dark ground, or under the eyelid of a closed eye. And those cases are too common to be disputed in which sensation continues to be felt in limbs that have been amputated.

To me it is very doubtful whether such sensations can rightly be called imaginary. There is no physical proof that they are not actual, but rather the contrary; for it can be shown that in all such cases there is an actual excitation of the neurility of a nerve.

They can only be called imaginary when the act of *inference* which accompanies them excludes, or only partially accepts, the counter-evidence of other senses. This is the case in any strong cerebral excitement whenever the faculty of inference becomes deranged, and a single sensation is consequently suffered so to domineer over all others as to become hallucination.

Between hallucination, therefore, and intelligent perception, this would seem to be the practical difference: intelligent perception qualifies the assertion of each sensation by comparing it with the testimony of all others; in hallucination, this power of comparison has become either imperfect or impossible, so that purely subjective sensation is attributed to an *object* which only exists in the imagination. This is generally the case in sleep, where sensation is almost invariably subjective, yet never consciously so; dreams being only the efforts of the imagination or the understanding to account objectively for subjective sensation.

It has been ascertained that the image even of an object in motion will remain on the retina, and continue to excite sensation in the nervous centre of the optic apparatus long after the object itself has been removed from the eye. And the sight of a horrible object will often haunt us for days or weeks, or a yet longer time after the horrible object has ceased to be substantially before us. The duration of the spectre will in that case be probably proportioned to the horror occasioned by the object which has caused it, that is to say, to the shock upon the mind. But the shock upon the 'mind, if excessive or permanent, may react upon the body. A horrible sensation produces a horrible idea; the horrible idea reproduces a horrible sensation.

Here it is obvious that all physiological inquiry touches very closely upon the domain of psychology. The practical physician can not refuse his serious attention to that great region of all inquiry into the complicated nature of human consciousness. For there is a constant interchange between sensation and thought, between action and contemplation, between the outward and the inward, between objects and ideas, between mind and matter. This is the point to which I have wished to bring inquiry, or on which, at least, I would fix conjecture.

I dismiss from present consideration all those spectral phenomena of which the cause can be distinctly traced to conditions purely physical, such as the black dog of the Cardinal Crescentius and the like. These are nearly always amenable to médicaments and regimen. For similar reasons I need not notice any of the current accounts of places supposed to be haunted. Whether these be old wives' fables or authenticated facts, they are equally removed from the scope of medical speculation, and have no interest for the present inquiry, which is solely concerned with the permanent relations between thought and sensation.

I assume a strong affection of the mind, either as

cause or effect, in its relation to the action of a man;
for example, of a criminal.

Let us suppose some passion to have taken possession of this man's mind.

That passion henceforward determines the course
of his actions to the exclusion of all normal manifest-
ations of the man's free will. It becomes to him, so
to speak, a *fatum* or destiny.

A human life obstructs the path of this passion.
Passion marches straight to its object, and tolerates no
obstacle by the way. Assassination has become a
necessary step on the path prescribed to the man by
the passion to which he has abdicated his will. The
man avoids with horror the thought of this, which in
turn pursues, and never quits him till it has made him
familiar with its presence. Occasion puts the knife
into his hand. The victim falls.

From the series of criminal thoughts issues the criminal act; from the abstract, the concrete. The murderer awakes from his long dream of murder with the
bloody knife in his hand.

The series of criminal thoughts belonged to the domain of one man's imagination; the bloody knife belongs to the domain of reality for all men.

Here the line is indicated which unites two points
whereof each is stationed in a different world.

Let A be the ideal world, and B the real world.

A has conducted to B.

Therefore B conducts to A.

That is to say, reality conducts to imagination, action to vision. But as, in the parallelogram of forces,
the action here is the resultant of the various activi-

ties contained in the imagination (*i. e.*, the series of criminal thoughts), so the imagination, when acted on in turn, can take no other form than that which it has itself determined. And, either permanently or periodically, the murderer (supposing of course the case, as previously assumed, to be one of hallucination) renews the action in the vision, which shows him the bloody knife, and the victim's corpse, etc.

The vision exists for the actor, but for him *only*. Consequently, without preceding *action*, no permanent or periodical *vision* is possible. The series of criminal thoughts alone, without result of any kind in action (an A without a B), can not produce permanent or periodical spectres. At least I know of no such case. The blot upon the brain becomes palpable to the bodily eye only when the darkness of it has passed into the deed which stains a life.

The great poet of the English Commonwealth says well:

> "Evil into the mind of God or man
> May come and go, so unapproved, and leave
> No spot or blame behind."*

* Were it not (as the dates sufficiently establish) that the doctor's speculations on this subject were written in the year 1836, I should certainly have surmised (notwithstanding a certain extravagance in his conclusions, to which a physiologist like Mr. Lewes would, no doubt, strongly demur) that he had previously read with attention that captivating work, "The Physiology of Common Life."

The dates, however, stubbornly forbid any such supposition.—*Verbum Sap.*—THE EDITOR.

CHAPTER V.

THEORY CONFOUNDED BY FACT.

IT is not without blushes that I now place on record this somewhat silly ebullition of the vanity of juvenile speculation ; but, at the time when I wrote the words just cited, the arrogant ardor of youth persuaded me that I had therein found safe foundation for a system of scientific thought; and yet, within a few weeks afterward, half a dozen pencil-marks scrawled by a stranger's hand on a piece of crumpled paper, blown into my possession by the wind of accident, sufficed to place me in perplexity and mistrust before my barely-acquired conviction.

In that scrap of paper had I not before my eye proof positive that Count R—— was under the dreadful dominion of some periodical apparition independent of his will? But was it possible to believe that the noble and imposing countenance of the count was simply a grimace assumed by a long-studied duplicity to mask the vulgar nature of a common criminal?

No, I could not do this. My whole mind indignantly revolted from such a suspicion. My theory, or this man's face—which was the liar?

A fico for all the theories that ever were invented, if they theorize away man's wholesome faith in man!

But what then, in a soul so pure and lofty as that

which seemed to reign royally at ease upon the open forehead of this strange being, could have occasioned effects so like the barking of a coward conscience at the memory of a crime?

Impossible to conceive! To me, at least, impossible.

Once more the life of this man seemed to thrust itself upon my own, and this time with an imperious pretension to enter into the inmost circle of those ideas to the service of which I had dedicated my intelligence.

What had before allured me with the charm of a vague curiosity now impelled me with a command almost like that of a duty.

I felt bound to find again this mysterious personage; to enter his inner life as he had entered mine; and to initiate myself into his secret with all the arrogated rights of a lawful claimant to an idea, who has been unjustly ousted from his due possession.

But my search was in vain.

I inquired at all the embassies; I inquired of the police; I inquired at the public hotels and the principal shops in Paris; and I utterly failed to find out any thing about Count R——.

I was at last forced to give up all hope of tracing him. He had probably left Paris.

Besides, the day fixed for my own departure was near at hand, and my friends declared it to be absolutely incumbent on me not to quit the French capital without having duly visited all the wonders of it.

I am sorry and ashamed to say that I had not the moral courage to resist this stupid imposition, and my last days, therefore, were devoted to what is called "sight-seeing."

When I recall the days that are past, I am conscious of having submitted to so much needless discomfort and infructuous toil from a lazy inability to resist this sort of pretensions, that, bitterly lamenting the precious hours I have too often squandered in the payment of illegal imposts to unwarrantable prejudice, I am resolved for the future to prove myself a very Hampden in the matter of all such unjustifiable exactions. When I think of all I have suffered, and all that humanity is still suffering for the want of some Hampden-hearted man to vindicate the cause of individual freedom against this most odious of all direct taxes—the sight-seeing tax, which is a tax upon the eyes of a man—*tumet jecur!* my gorge rises, and the spleen of my just indignation—overflows into—

CHAPTER VI.

ADVICE TO SIGHT-SEERS.

AFTER long stay in any place, in the moment when we are about to leave it, one thinks it a duty to see, in the most desperate hurry, every thing in that place which one has had no care to see at one's leisure.

Monuments, museums, parks, public buildings, collections—every thing, from prisons to pagodas, puts on the obnoxious form of a tax collector, and comes knocking at the doors of that respectable mansion, for which conscience already pays a sufficiently high rent to convention.

In that fretful, flurried, unsettling moment of man's fugitive life, when he is paying his bills and packing up his portmanteau, then is the time, of all others, when these importunate notorieties take mean advantage of his helpless condition, and voiciferously insist on a visit. There is no appeasing them but by submissive compliance with their demands; for they turn even our very friends into an army of touters.

And we call this—"seeing the curiosities of the place."

Yet I can conceive of no objects which a man should be less curious to see than those of which he knows beforehand that he will never see them again. Oh that "wallet" of time, "wherein he puts alms for Oblivion!" Oh the things we stuff (and with what haste!) into that lumber-room of passing impressions, from which Memory can never afterward fetch away a stick of serviceable furniture!

Animi fenestræ oculi. How do we fritter and dribble away this grand capital of sight! For sight is a capital, and it is not inexhaustible. How do we impoverish the exchequer of the eye by changing golden ingots into copper coins for the purchase of an infinite number of things of farthing value! How will ye rise in the retrospect of judgment against us, all ye lost looks and squandered glances! Poor, wasted pocket-money of that rich spendthrift, Want-of-thought! Thefts from the sacred heritage of Beauty maladministered by idle hours, untrustworthy guardians of a property not theirs!

Oh dear Reader, if in the hour of thy departure from any place thine eye hath yet left a look to spare, give it rather to thy neighbor's dog; for he at least, in some sort, will render thee the worth of it by a last friendly wag of his tail; but hang it not up, like a worn-out garment never to be used again, on the stony, callous cornice of some monument dedicated by the impatience of a moment to the importunity of Oblivion.

Is it not distressing to see men of a sober conduct, in the last moment of leaving a place where, for so many months or years, they have lived at ease and in dignity, suddenly plagued with this sight-seeing fever, "grin like a dog, and run to and fro in the city?"

If you ask them why they do this, they have no better answer than that "every body does it."

What a frightful, invisible tyrant is this Every

Body, who respects not the humble independence of Any Body!

Well, if thou canst, content thee with this Αὐτὸς. ἔφα of the modern Pythagoreans. But as for me, *eheu! eheu!* what has it not cost me—what sweat! what toil!—in the going up and down of interminable stairs! whereby, *me Hercle!* I believe that I have exuded in the sweat of my brow many thousand shillingworths of knowledge, for which, may the generation of guides and door-keepers, if they be not condemned to hard labor at the stone of Sisyphus on my account, remember me favorably to their fellow Charons of a better world!

As for those modern Pythagoreans, whenever by his *ipse dixit* I now detect one of them, I fear him as a man infected with a contagious disease. *Fœnum habet in cornu.* I take the alarm, and avoid that man by all means in my power, inwardly praying (since I would not be uncharitable) that it may graciously please Providence to remove him speedily from this world, and, if possible, take him to itself.

Mayst thou also, oh dear Reader, be ever able on all such occasions to exclaim "*Sic me servabit Apollo;*" and whenever thou shalt be pestered by these false prophets crying "Lo here!" and "Lo there!" may Heaven send thee grace to withstand them!

CHAPTER VII.

THE GAMBLING-HOUSE IN THE RUE ——.

THUS one evening, the programme arranged by some of my friends for the curiosity which they imputed to my sense of duty happened to lead me to a place which I had never before visited, and which (I admit) merits one visit, but not two—to wit, a gambling-house.

It was one of those fashionable hells, which, at the time I am speaking of, were tolerated at Paris, and which, I am sorry to say, are to be found to-day in almost every German watering-place. The house in the Rue —— differed in no particular from the generality of those splendid temples of Fortune which assuredly need no description. But to me the scene I witnessed there was new, and, truth to say, it was not exactly what I had expected. To my thinking one essential element is wanting to the passion for play, namely, grandeur. Indeed, this feverish cupidity has nothing in common with passion except insatiability, and for this reason it does not seem to me to merit the noble name of passion.

Ambition, Love, nay, even Inebriety, when it has not yet quite brutalized its victim, do in a certain sense, and to a certain extent, enlarge and exalt the faculties of those who yield to them, or else, at least, they force

E

those faculties to produce themselves in some new and unusual form. With this it is otherwise. The player himself, indeed, may be violently agitated by the stupendous hazard of Fortune, which at one moment uplifts him on its topmost wave, and at another moment sinks him suddenly to the abyss. In the rapid alternation of triumph and despair, thus tossed to and fro between power and impuissance even to the point of insensibility, the mind of the gambler may perhaps present to him the image of himself as something Titanic and supermortal. But to the spectator he presents only the vile grimace of an assumed composure, which is neither natural nor admirable, or else yet the more painful image of a demoniac whose convulsion, under possession, can inspire no other feeling than repugnance.

I was already about to turn away disgusted, when the remarks exchanged among a crowd of spectators like myself, who had collected round the table for *Trente et Quarante*, attracted my attention, and induced me to join the group.

"'Pristie! He has put on Red for the fifteenth time, and won!"

I pushed my own with difficulty into the crowd of heads that were turned in the direction where, on the opposite side of the table, was seated the player, whose successful fidelity to a single color had so greatly excited the admiration of the onlookers.

A heap of gold, piles of rouleaux and notes, left me no doubt where to look for the favorite of Fortune.

Hardly could I repress a cry of astonishment on recognizing Count R——.

This time his appearance reminded me more vivid-
ly than ever of the scene on board the steam-boat,
when the coldness and fixity of his features, compared
with the violent play of the boiling waters, had so
strangely impressed me; for at this moment I could
not but similarly contrast with the tumult of passions
visible in the human waves that were fluctuating all
round him, the same impassive, imperturbable quies-
cence on the face of that man.

The cards had just been shuffled for a new cut.
Strongly impressed by a sense of the certainty with
which the strange player seemed to carry fortune with
him, the majority of the *Ponte* followed his example;
and, as he did not yet seem willing to pocket his
gains, new stakes covered that part of the table which,
for the sixteenth time, had been so decisively favored
by luck.

Just at the moment, however, when the croupier
cried, " *Le jeu est fait : rien ne va plus,*" the immense
heap of gold and notes whose proprietor by his per-
sistent adherence to Red had seduced all the other
players to set their stakes on the same color, was
swiftly, almost imperceptibly, pushed across, on to the
side of the contrary chance. Taken completely with
surprise by this rapid movement, the other players let
slip the decisive moment when, by following that
movement, they also might have saved their money.

For, this time, Red lost, Black won.

The stranger, already so admired for his constant
good luck, had, by one of those instantaneous inspira-
tions which are quite inexplicable, made Fortune his
slave for the seventeenth time, and realized the high-

est sum which the bank remained in a condition to
pay!

Every Body was astonished. I myself, who had
witnessed the whole operation, was at a loss to explain
this instantaneous change of plan on the part of the
player.

I had not for one moment taken my eyes off the
count. I was paralyzed and confounded by the conflicting testimony of my own senses, which on the one
hand affirmed that the stakes had been moved, and, on
the other hand, that the player, whom I had been
watching with intense attention, had never once stirred from the position in which he was sitting with
folded arms, apparently quite unconcerned with the
game.

It seemed impossible that he himself could have
moved the stakes without my having noticed the action. But, if not he, who then could have moved
them?

Every Body present must have been convinced that
they were moved by the player himself; for nobody
raised a single objection; and even the croupiers, who
have the eyes of Argus, did not challenge the fairness
and legality of the operation.

It is true that I was so occupied in watching the
count's face that I did not pay much attention to the
table; and, though I am ready to swear that I did not
see him move, I do not feel authorized to swear that
I saw him *not* move. For certainly I saw the gold
change places; and what must make me think that I
was at that moment under the effect of a strongly excited imagination is the fact that, in the instant of

transition from Red to Black, there seemed to me to flash out of the yellow heap a quick, quivering ray of violet light, like the sparkle of a jewel rapidly moved.

But my impressions of that moment may well have been confused, for immediately all was in uproar and horror on every side. The croupiers started up; the players, who had lost their last stake, and were hurrying angrily away, stopped short, and stared with alarmed faces at the Silesian.

His countenance had become overspread with the pallor of death, and transfigured with terror. His eyes were starting from their sockets. His lips were blue and hideous. I saw his body, rigid as a corpse, sway heavily forward from the chair in which he was seated. The next moment he was stretched upon the floor insensible.

CHAPTER VIII.

THE DOOR OF THE SECRET.

THE count was carried unconscious into the adjoining room. I followed. When I mentioned that I was a physician, every body made way for me. I was afraid of apoplexy, and judged it necessary to let blood immediately. I never go any where without my lancet-case. At my request the count was placed upon a sofa. I bared his arm, applied the bandages, and made the necessary operation. When I had no farther need of assistance every body withdrew. I was left alone with my patient. All was silent.

At last, at last, I was at the door of the secret! Would it open to me?

For the first time, I was enabled to contemplate, unwitnessed, undisturbed, the tissue of noble lines which composed that beautiful proud face on which the semblance of death had now set its solemn seal.

Before me lay—an open book, but hard to read, and writ in mystic characters—the history of a profound sorrow.

"No!" I murmured; "impossible! Never can crime have established its loathsome workshop behind that pure, fair brow. In the musical harmony of those perfect features I see no trace of that great discord—Vice."

The blood which I had let had relieved the head. The face of the count, though still pale, had resumed a natural hue. The horror had left his countenance. He lay there calm as an infant asleep. His features had relapsed into that expression of noble repose which they seemed to owe to nature rather than to art.

"What Spirit of Reproach," I mused, "can have glided, furtive from the other world, into this corporeal sphere, to execute in the soul of this man the office of the avenger?"

The more I examined the countenance on which I was gazing, the more did it inspire me with compassionate respect. There were lines upon the face which told of deep sorrow; but nothing mean, nothing vulgar.

"Vain," I muttered to myself, "vain and impuissant are the pity and commiseration of a feeble fellow-creature to arrest the retributive hand of Eternal Justice; but if it be only the toil of a too-sensitive self-scrutiny which has advanced thus perilously far that frontier which separates this visible material world from the realm of things unseen, then be thou sure, poor spirit, that there is one beside thee whose duty is to bring thee such aid as man may bring to man."

A deep sigh and a feeble movement of the patient announced the return of consciousness. I drew back softly. There was a profound silence which I did not dare to break.

After a short pause, the count lifted up the arm which I had not bandaged, and motioned me to approach him. I obeyed. He took my hand in his, and looked long and wistfully into my face. What-

ever was the object of this scrutiny, he seemed satisfied by the result of it. A faint smile broke over his
countenance, and, without either false embarrassment
or exaggerated cordiality, he addressed me in these
words:

"It is not for the first time, I think, that we now
see each other, and I have a certain presentiment it
will not be for the last time. I do not thank you.
Toward you, indeed, the observance of an empty cour-
tesy already appears to me too little; and yet more
than this would, at present, seem to me too much. I
wish you to do me the favor to accompany me home,
in order that you may, if you think it necessary, complete those good offices which you have already so
successfully commenced. I think I can now move
without difficulty."

Silently our hands clasped, and I left him to order
a *fiacre*.

In the next room I found the banker of the gambling-house, who, at my request, sent one of his servants to order a carriage from the nearest cab-stand. I
told the servant to wait for us with the carriage at the
side door, where we would join him by the back staircase, and was about to return to the count, when the
banker stopped me.

"Pardon! One word, if you please, Monsieur le
Docteur. The money?"

The door was half open, and the count, who had
heard this inquiry, rose before it was finished, and,
joining us, answered it himself.

"I regret," said he, turning to the banker, "the discomfort which I have involuntarily caused you."

Then turning to me, "Monsieur—and your name?"

I gave it.

He bowed and resumed. "Monsieur de V——
will have the goodness to call upon you to-morrow,
and dispose of half the money in accordance with my
wishes, which he will allow me to communicate to
him. The other half I request you to be good enough
to distribute among the servants of your establishment, to whom I fear I have occasioned some trouble."

The carriage was announced, and I entered it with
the count. We did not exchange a word on our way
to his hotel, which was in the Faubourg St. Germain,
a spacious apartment, *au premier*, which, with the ex-
ception of a few rare objects of art, had all the appearance of a house hired "ready furnished." The count
was evidently exhausted. His valet, who opened the
door to us, and in whom I recognized the old servant
I had before seen on board the steamer, did not speak
a word of French. I explained to him in German
that his master had had a slight accident, and gave
him the few orders which I considered necessary for
the night. The old man shook his head mournfully,
and muttered several times, "Again, dear God! again?
The Lord help us!"

I enjoined upon the count the most perfect repose.
A stupid counsel, which he received with an ironic
smile, and of which I myself felt the utter futility.

"Pray do me the favor," he said, as we shook hands,
"to let me see you again to-morrow."

I promised to call upon him the next day, and we
parted for that night.

"I wonder," I said to myself, as I left the house,
"whether I shall see again that woman's face."

CHAPTER IX.

Remains Shut.

The next day I waited on Count Edmond R——
at the hour which I had been impatiently expecting.
As I approached the house I looked eagerly at the
windows. No face at those windows; no Loreley
there with beckoning hand. The blinds were drawn.
Whatever sorrow inhabited those chambers had no
voice. My heart was listening, but I heard not the
note of the hautboy.

I was shown into a large saloon overlooking the
court. Not a flower in the windows; not a broidery
frame in the corner; not the ghost of a passing perfume; no bonnet, glove, or shawl upon the chair; no
careless piece of needle-work upon the table; no single gracious trace of a woman's presence, beautified
the cheerless aspect of that hideous formal furniture,
which remains a monument to the bad taste of the
"Great Empire."

Was she in this house? was she in Paris? or was
the count here quite alone?

I had not much time to look about me before Count
R—— entered the room. Holding out both his
hands, he came forward to meet me with gracious
cordiality. All trace of the previous night's excitement had completely disappeared from his face and

manner. It needed all that perspicuity which is only possessed by the practiced eye of the physician to en-able me to detect under this well-assumed mask of easy indifference the struggle maintained by the pow-er of a strong will against the effort of nature.

"You see in me," said the count, smiling, "a flat-tering testimonial to your skill and experience. Your excellent treatment has done wonders; and I owe to your successful care a calm night and refreshing sleep; the greatest blessing which the craft of science can filch from the thrift of nature. Be seated. I feel stron-ger and better than ever. In this you have done me a double service; for the fact is, that pressing affairs, which compelled me to fix my departure for to-day, would have seriously suffered had I been obliged to postpone my return to Silesia. To-day, however, I feel so well, that, knowing by experience the strength of my constitution, I have no reason to fear the effects of a journey. Instead of thanks, permit me, rather, to increase my debt to you by a request."

This manœuvre, by which the count obviously in-tended to prevent a closer approach upon my part, did not find me altogether unprepared. Before rejoining him that morning, I had reflected on what should be my line of conduct toward him, and what might pos-sibly be the character of his toward me. I was re-solved not to injure by any ill-timed or exaggerated advances the favorable impression on which chance (if chance it were) had enabled me to found the hope of future intimacy; and I felt persuaded that a man educated in all those refinements of life which render men's nature especially sensitive to the graces of little things, would instinctively shrink from the embrace of a clumsy cordiality.

Without betraying the least surprise or embarrassment, therefore, I immediately gave my consent to this proposal, which I could see to have been carefully prepared.

I could at once congratulate myself on the effect of my reply; for Count Edmond was not so completely master of his feelings (or did not care perhaps so completely to conceal them) but what I could seize, as it were, upon the wing, an expression of relief and satisfaction which flitted over his features.

"How enchanted I am," said he, "that we two, strangers as we are, so well understand each other!"

He cordially shook me by the hand, and I asked him for his last orders.

"No, no," he replied, with a frank and pleasant smile, "not *last*, my dear sir. There is no such thing as last. At least I don't think that either you or I have much belief in that word. However, if you will have it so, this is my last *request*. You heard me, last night, dispose of your good offices without even awaiting your permission, by informing the banker at ——'s that you would be kind enough to call upon him in my name for a sum of money, which I am ashamed of having acquired in such a way, and of which the possession would be most repugnant to all my feelings. Indeed, I can assure you that I am no gambler. Curiosity led me (perhaps like yourself) to that house. I wished to pay my entrance by a small stake, and I only left my money upon the table for the purpose of getting rid of it. The rest you know."

He paused. His lip quivered for a moment, but he quickly resumed:

"In telling me your name, you recalled to my mind various associations which had hitherto attached themselves *only* to your name; for till then my good fortune had not favored me with the pleasure of your personal acquaintance. Your name, however, had often been mentioned to me by friends of your mother's family, with whom I am slightly acquainted. I know the noble object of your life, and I have even been sometimes disposed to envy you the rewards of an existence so devoted to the welfare of others.

"Well, now, you see, I am going to intrude my participation upon this good work of yours. Favor me by accepting this small sum, and applying it to the relief of that poverty and suffering to the cause of which you have so generously dedicated your endeavors; and which, indeed, without your skill and sympathy, this slight offering of mine would be powerless to alleviate. And hereafter—"

I was going to speak, but he interrupted me, and went on rapidly:

"Hereafter, whenever you fall in with such cases of need as you may consider deserving, pray do not fail to regard me as your banker. Two lines from you to L——, near Breslau, with the address of the sufferer, will enable you to make at least *one* person happy, if not two. And now adieu! We shall meet again. I feel it, without stopping at this moment to consider how or where."

He shook me once more by the hand, and thus we took leave of each other.

Once more this strange figure receded from my sight into unknown distance; and the solution of the enigma on which I had thought to touch slipped from my grasp, and left me as ignorant as I had been before.

This time, however, I felt that a sort of link had been established between myself and this man—a link which time and distance might perhaps attenuate, but could not wholly dissolve.

CHAPTER X.

HOME!

I EXECUTED with great satisfaction the last orders of Count R——. I only knew too well what to do with the money. Within my experience of this brilliant holiday Paris, there was no lack of tears to dry nor of misery to mitigate. My own affairs did not detain me much longer in this town, which I was already impatient to leave. Nothing is more fatiguing than the days and weeks which precede an anticipated and inevitable departure.

I hailed with joy the hour which found me, on the stroke of six in the afternoon, before the great courtyard in the Rue Jean Jacques Rousseau.

Oh, happy days of most unvalued quiet, too rashly and too cheaply sold to the army of railway contractors in exchange for sixty miles an hour and spine diseases! days when life enjoyed the dignity of delay, when the world traveled by post, and the world's wife on a pillion! Then, as we jogged along the highway, I do verily believe that (in despite of Danton's ghost) high and low, rich and poor, wise and foolish, stood far enough asunder to be able to take a good look at each other as they passed along, and, as one says, "knew their places." Now the journey of life is more rapid, but I'll be shot if I think it half so pleasant; for in the hurry-skurry we are so tumbled to-

gether, that who can say where he is or where he will
be; and 'tis but a sorry chance which of us may fall
uppermost.

Six! It clashes clear from the great dial, and the
frosty twilight is falling.

Six! And cheerily issues the first britska from the
inner court, where these ponderous locomotives of an
unlocomotive age used to lurk harnessed and ready
when the hour struck to disperse themselves leisurely
to the four quarters of the compass.

Bordeaux! shouts the *employé de la poste*. A couple
of travelers jump into the carriage. The door shuts
with a sharp click. The postillion blithely clacks his
long-lashed, short-handled whip, and four colossal *per-
cherons* strain forward in the traces, and start off at a
brisk trot to the merry sound of a multitude of little
tinkling bells.

Calais! Lyons! A second *calèche;* a third.

The *courrier* swings himself into the *cabriolet.* They
are off.

At last, Strasbourg! How my heart beats! *O
dulce germen matris!* (may the souls of the gramma-
rians forgive me the pun!) Oh dear mother German!
Home! and with what homeward thoughts I scale
the high carriage step. We issue on to the great open
spaces of the night by the Barrier St. Denis. I plunge
my yearning looks beyond me, deep and far into the
glimmering air, searching on the utmost verge of the
dark horizon that long line of clouds which may perhaps o'ercanopy (oh pleasant thought!) the skies of
Germany. And as the restless roar of Paris (that
never quiet heart) sinks faint behind me on the seri-

ous, cold night air, I have little care to remember that
I am leaving, perhaps forever, a world bottomless,
vast—a world of vice and grandeur, of the ludicrous
and the sublime.

PART II.

THE PATIENT.

To tread a maze that never shall have end,
To burn in sighs and starve in daily tears,
To climb a hill and never to descend,
Giants to kill, and quake at childish fears,
To pine for food, and watch th' Hesperian tree,
To thirst for drink, and nectar still to draw,
To live accurs'd, whom men hold bless'd to be,
And weep those wrongs which never creature saw.

HENRY CONSTABLE.

BOOK I.

A Seed from the Tomb.

The story of my life,
And the particular accidents gone by.
Tempest, Act V.

BOOK I.

CHAPTER I.

ANNO DOMINI Eighteen Hundred and Forty-two.

In the heart of Silesia, in the good town of Breslau, any body you may meet in the streets there will be able to show you the way to the doctor's house; and if you care to see again an old acquaintance, come here. Come winter or summer, when you will, sure of welcome. The guest-chamber is ever ready. You shall have the best room in the house; not without a gust of apple-blossoms at the window if you come when the swallows are here, nor a merry twitter of redbreasts (old accustomed guests of mine) if you wait for the snow and frost. The best room in the house, did I say? nay, but you shall have the two best rooms in the house, if you will bring your wife with you; for since we parted at Paris, oh very dear Reader, I, at least, am no longer a bachelor. My life is quieted and completed by the peaceful presence of a wise, kind woman-face—a face that makes itself more felt than seen. And there are little chirping voices about the rooms here. So, then, if you also bring with you any of that pleasant, provoking, noisy, busy little baggage, so much the better. We will shut it all up in the nursery, where all day long it is full of the most important business, jumping and skipping up and down, and sliding about with sprawling foot and hand, and building palaces with chairs and cushions, and driving coaches, and blowing trumpets, and making to itself a hundred Iliads.   For this is the Heroic Age.

Only, in truth, I would not have had you choose for the date of your visit that wild night of St. Sylvester, when this year of our Lord Eighteen Hundred and Forty-two was knocking, in snow and storm, at the creaking doors of Time.   Sharply and bitterly— not in welcome, not in love—the Old Year, in his dying hour, snorted with icy breath in the face of his young usurper.   Well may he have been muttering from his chappy lip, "Turn back! turn back, ill-omened brother!   Set not thy fatal foot upon this poor distracted planet, for in thy dry and shining eyes I see the glare of fire and of famine.   Thy hands are empty of the tilth, and the tithe thou hast consecrated to Death!"

But the New Year turned not back.

It turned not back before the gates of Hamburg, where the blithe bells rang with unsuspicious peals its treacherous entry into that devoted town—bells soon made to ring far other music, when the midnight was bright with the glare and hot with the breath of the Destroying Angel; for then, swung fiercely by the unseen hands of the Spirits of Fire, they rang their own death-knell; rang till, from their pious habitations and pure lives of gentle motion and sweet sound, they dropped, deformed dumb things; rang till the burning metal trickled and crawled like boiling blood among their ruined homes, and became again dead earthy ore in earth.*

The New Year turned not back. It turned not back before the snow-capped forest-hills of Bohemia, whose greenest saplings had but lately shed such merry lustre in cottage and in palace, decked by young hands, to celebrate the blessed Christmas-time. Less merry a light was yours, old father pines, that rested in the forest! For nine days long the smoke of your burning overshadowed two kingdoms, and for nine nights long the glare of your fires made pale the stars of heaven, while the timid deer sought willingly the hunter's door.

It turned not back, that stern New Year, before many a threshold which Death had marked for sorrow. My own it passed with mourning and a mother's loss.

Long here in German land shall we remember thee, not lovingly, ill-fated year! Ay! till bells on Hamburg towers rebuilt ring in some better time; ay! till the ashes of those burnt forests pass again to living green; ah me! till Death with other kinder touchings has stopped the bleeding wounds in hearts which thou hast stricken.

Not upon this Sylvester's night, then, would I have had thee come, dear Reader, to test my hospitality. Not here, indeed, wouldst thou have found me, but by the lonely sick-bed of a dying man; not amid

* One of the strangest phenomena of the great fire of Hamburg was the seemingly spontaneous ringing of the bells, occasioned by the disturbance of the heated air.

F

merry little faces keeping holiday, but with prayer
and supplication (the only medicine poured for him),
keeping watch beside a long-outwearied spirit, whose
sole physician was a friend.   For there, upon that bed
under which already the grave was yawning, lay
stretched (much needing rest) the tired frame of Edmond Count R——.

CHAPTER II.

AN UNEXPECTED VISITOR.

AFTER leaving Paris I temporarily established myself in Berlin, a place of residence which I selected for the ready access it afforded me to those great reservoirs of physical suffering called hospitals, as well as for the intellectual atmosphere for which the Prussian capital is renowned. Not long, however, after I had pitched my tent amid the Brandenburg sands, I received and accepted an invitation from Breslau to take the chair of the medical professorship at that University. Here I was fortunate enough to succeed in soon securing a connection which assured to me an easy, if not a brilliant future.

Among the writings by which, immediately after my return from Paris, I had sought to introduce myself to the literary world in Germany was a small pamphlet entitled

A TREATISE

UPON

SPECTRAL APPARITIONS,

BEING

A CONTRIBUTION

TO THE

PHENOMENOLOGY OF THE BRAIN.

It fell still-born, however, and nearly ruined my publishers, who were not men of capital.* Those of the τì νέον; class, who sought to stimulate a jaded imagination by new incredibilities, found the book flat and insipid; those, on the other hand, who were the constituted guardians of a languid experience, denounced it as flighty and fantastic. Thus the work failed to conciliate any portion of the public; and I myself, amid the occupations of a daily-increasing practice, had almost entirely forgotten this early failure of my literary efforts, when it was suddenly recalled to my recollection by the event which I am about to relate.

One night, I had returned home later than usual from the house of a patient, and was still engaged in my study, when my servant announced that there was a strange gentleman in the hall who was anxious to speak with me.

It was long past midnight; but a physician is bound to receive all visitors at all hours, and I bade the servant tell the stranger I would see him at once.

He entered.

It was an old man of lofty stature but drooping carriage. The dim, uncertain light from under the shade of my lamp did not enable me to distinguish his features immediately, but he had scarcely uttered a word before I recognized Count R———.

I recognized him by his voice. In that shadowy light I should have hardly recognized him by any

---

* I hope, both for my own sake and that of the highly-respected firm who have undertaken the protection of it, that the doctor's present invasion of the literary world may be less ill fated.—Editor.

other indication. It was many years since we had last met, and he was grievously altered. There are some men who preserve the aspect of youth to the extreme limit of middle age; then they seem to grow old in a year, and, as if Old Age, having finally overcome his victim, was exasperated into taking vengeance upon those features which had so long resisted his attack, these men collapse into a decrepitude which is quite disproportioned to the number of their years.

The aspect of Count Edmond R—— was like that of a broken statue. It was the painful union of beauty and ravage. His hair was still luxuriant, but snow-white. His face was plowed with deep furrows. There was a hopeless droop about the lines of the mouth. His gait and manner still preserved much of their old stateliness, but it was the stateliness of resignation— the dignity of a defeated man. His whole face and figure had but one expression—intense fatigue.

"If," said the count, after we had exchanged a few commonplace salutations rendered painful by our mutual embarrassment, "if to-night I seek you once more, it is not to slip out of your hands as formerly. Shall I own to you that when we first casually encountered each other on the deck of that steam-boat years (how many years?) ago, I was vexed and displeased by the pertinacious scrutiny of your regard? Accustomed, however, to let pass all such impressions without allowing them to disturb my habitual equanimity, I was surprised that I could not, in this instance, entirely rid my mind of the recollection of that passing encounter, nor shake off the peculiar, but indefinite sensation which I first experienced on perceiving that your attention was fixed on me. It was not an agreeable sensation, nor one which I wished to prolong; and a few years afterward, when I twice came unexpectedly and unwillingly upon you—when I twice found in you (and that, I am well assured, without any premeditation upon your part) an un-summoned witness to scenes in which you saw me under deep emotion, I began to surmise that it might possibly be something more than blind chance which thus seemed to insist on establishing relations between two persons so far removed from each other by the ordinary circumstances of life. For before we met again at the hell in the Rue ——, I had detected (though too late) your presence on a spot where I had believed myself utterly alone—by the Mare d'Auteuil. Since then, I have frequently felt myself impelled to approach you, either by the inward voice of my des-tiny, or perhaps only by the vulgar desire to clear up what I conceived to be an error. But ever I have hesitated and hung back rather than risk a step which might perhaps prove destructive to a certain dumb hope that has long since become a sort of consolatory custom to my thoughts, and to which I am constrained to cling with a confidence derived from despair in other sources of comfort.

"This last attempt, therefore, I have put off as long as it was in my power to do so. That it is no longer in my power to refrain from it is proved by my pres-ence in your house to-night."

I can not attempt to describe to you the sort of shudder with which I listened to these words. They were uttered quite simply, and without any symptom of extraordinary emotion. But precisely on this account—precisely in proportion to the simplicity of the speech itself, and the unaffected frankness of the avowal thus made by a man whom I knew to be both sensitively proud and a consummate master in the art of repressing his emotions, I felt a sudden repugnance to receive the confession which he now seemed resolved to impose upon my confidence. Any such act of confidence upon his part had been so long withheld—any such avowal of weakness must, I felt assured, have been wrung from such a desperate conviction of defeat, that this consideration, added to the sense of apprehension and dismay with which I was affected by the accents of a voice which vibrated strangely under the weight of an excessive melancholy, seemed to give to the decision which I might be called upon to pronounce respecting facts yet unknown to me a responsibility too solemn to be lightly undertaken. The moment which I had once ardently desired was come. I was afraid of it. I shrank back and remained silent. I could not belie the gravity of my own feelings by the utterance of any commonplace assurances.

He seemed to understand this; for, as though he had not expected any reply, he continued after a momentary pause,

"A thousand circumstances of seemingly small account," he said, "combined to urge me unceasingly upon the path which was destined to bring me here. As though half the world were in a conspiracy to bring us together, seldom a year would pass by but what your name reached me from the most unexpect-

ed quarters, and always in some such way as seemed
to place you, maugre my own disinclination, in strange
and significant intercourse with my mind.

"One of those chances became at last decisive—one
of those chances which must remain inexplicable if we
do not regard them as whispers from that mysterious
Prompter who forces us dull players to perform the
parts assigned to us in the Great Tragedy of Human
Life."

His voice faltered a moment, but he hastily resumed:

"My bookseller sends me periodically the new
books of the season. One day my glance fell carelessly upon the printed wrappage of one of those par-
cels which I had not yet opened. My attention was
instantly arrested and absorbed by these words: '*The
vision exists for the actor, but for him only. It presupposes his action. The series of criminal thoughts alone,
without result of any kind in action (an A without a B)
can not produce permanent or periodical apparitions. At
least I know of no such case.*' Perhaps you have looked deep enough into my life to divine the impression
which these words made upon me. If an oracle had
appeared upon the wall in characters of fire, such a
miracle could not have so profoundly affected me as
this dry reflection of another human mind upon a
piece of printed paper. I sent instantly for the work
from which this sheet had been torn. Eagerly I turned to the title-page. The author's name was on it.
The author's name was yours. Since then, your book
has become the constant companion of my thoughts."

He stopped abruptly, and seemed almost overpowered. I could not answer him. With an obvious effort, he continued:

"I will come at once to the object of my visit here to-night. That case which was wanting to your experience—"

Again he stopped, and pressed his hand to his forehead as though he felt his brow must burst with the surrender of a secret now for the first time wrenched from the deepest roots of a life.

"That case," he repeated, "which you failed to find, I offer it to you. I would place it in your hands, for I feel my end approach. If the knowledge of evil can serve the cause of good, be it yours to dispose of. Spare me the pain of being myself your guide along that thorny path over which the bleeding traces of a tired pilgrim will suffice to point the way. These papers—take them; read them."

He rose, placed a packet of papers in my hand and his address, bowed, and hurriedly turned to the door.

"One question!" I exclaimed. "The countess?"

Suddenly his whole stature rose its full height. He turned round and stood before me erect, solemn, almost awful. He lifted his hand, and looking upward with a strange expression on his countenance, said, "Yonder, at the right hand of her husband."

F 2

CHAPTER III.

THE SECRET IN MY HANDS AT LAST.

NOTHING but my own unquiet footsteps broke the profound silence of the night. I was alone. For more than an hour I continued pacing up and down the room in strong excitement, weighing in my hand that pregnant packet which I dared not open till I had composed the trouble of those emotions to which my unexpected interview with the count had given rise.

By degrees I grew calmer; but it was nearly morning before I sat down, with something of judicial solemnity, to open those "sessions of silent thought" from which Edmond Count R—— had invoked the verdict on his life.

Letters in various handwritings (chiefly a woman's), memoranda, pages of a journal, made up the contents of the packet which the count had placed in my hands. I read them in the order in which I found them; but a due regard for the patience and convenience of other readers (no doubt less interested than myself) compels me to reduce the substance of these documents to a summary, reserving only the permission to extract *in extenso* some of the original papers which appear to be specially important.

CHAPTER IV.

EARLY DAYS.

THE peasant sees it, for a moment, from the river, when he floats his raft down the rapid waters of the Weidnitz; for there the river winds, and the trees are thick. The reaper sees it all day long, envying, perhaps, the shadow and the cool of it, when the sun is hot upon the red corn-lands beyond the woody upland slopes. It is an old chateau that has seen many changes, and suffered few. A massive pile of gray stone, with tall copper roofs, built four-square about a quiet court. There the grass has a will of its own, and pushes its way, under trying circumstances, between the chinks in the much-flawed pavement. There, too, the sun-dial is always conspicuous, but the sun seldom. The south front is flanked by a square, flat garden (Italian style), with long, straight walks, whereto you descend from a broad terrace by a flight of stone stairs. The garden leads to a bowling-alley. In the middle of the garden is a fish-tank, full of old red fish and old black water. Beyond this is the park. It is not like your English parks, but rather a sort of slovenly meadow, which rambles astray in all directions, and finally loses itself in the great woodland all round. There you may hunt the roebuck, the red deer even, and the wild boar. Such a place for shooting and for fishing never was. For about all this the river puts its arm, lovingly and quietly, like an old friend.

This is the first scene which shapes itself before my mind's eye as I read. It is the chateau of L——. And here, at ease with his family, dwells Arthur Count R——, a wealthy, high-bred, honorable, kind-hearted, perhaps somewhat weak-minded nobleman. Count Arthur married late in life. It was a love marriage, however, and, what is yet more rare, a happy one. Three children were born of this marriage. Edmond, the first-born, who for some time remained the only child, for he was four years old when his brother Felix was born. To Felix succeeded, two years afterward, a sister, Marie. Marie was sickly from birth, and died at three years old. The more complete had been the happiness of the countess, the more violent was her grief for the loss of her only daughter. Heaven, however, accorded her a compensation for this loss. The earliest and tenderest friend of the countess (the companion of her childhood) had been wedded young, very young, to the spendthrift Prince C——, in Bohemia. She died in the first year of her marriage, giving birth to a daughter; and her last request to her husband was that this infant might be confided to the care of her friend, the wife of Count Arthur R——, in Silesia.

This sacrifice was not made without reluctance by the widower. But the prince, whatever may have been his faults, had been attached to his wife, and was deeply affected by her death. He felt himself pledged to fulfill his promise to the princess on her death-bed. Besides, how was it possible for a young man, devoted to pleasure, to look after the infant thus left on his hands? So little Juliet was conducted to L——, and henceforth became a member of the count's family. The prince soon forgot his double loss in a life of debauchery at Vienna. In a few years he ran through his fortune; and one morning, finding himself with empty pockets, after an enforced settlement with his creditors, he accepted active service in the Imperial army, and fell at Aspern at the head of his regiment.

Count Arthur, as guardian of the orphan, secured to Juliet all that could be saved from the wreck of her father's fortune; and the little girl, who had no recollection of any other home, grew up at L—— with the two boys, regarded by the members of the count's family as one of themselves, and accustomed to regard them in return with all the affection of a sister and daughter.

Juliet was a charming child, essentially loveable, because essentially loving. All the conditions of her adopted home were of a nature to develop the great feature of her character—trustfulness.

The education of Edmond had been completed at home under paternal care.

I have no personal experience of your English public schools; but I have always regarded them as the great reservoirs of the English character. What seems to me the main defect of our German system of education is that it is too exclusively confined to intellectual development. The motive power of man does not exist in the intellectual, but in the moral qualities. The *quantula sapientia* that governs mankind has been a subject of continual wonder to the contemplative portion of the human community. But the explanation of this apparent phenomenon is probably to be found in a fact too commonly ignored, and yet hardly to be disputed, viz., that the governing qualities are moral rather than intellectual. Our lives, and our influence upon the lives of others, are much less dependent upon intellectual superiority than is generally supposed. It is a common saying that Knowledge is Power; but the kind of knowledge thereby implied requires definition. Perhaps it would be more generally true to say Power is Knowledge. It can not in any case be asserted that book-learning is power. The chief object of education should not be the accumulation of information, but the formation of character; and I know of no system of education by which this object is so well attained as that of the English public schools.

It is not so much acuteness of the dialectic faculty, high culture, or extended range of contemplation, that governs mankind, but rather energy, sympathy, perseverance, conciliation, enthusiasm. And in all the practical affairs of life, even men of the highest intellect must probably rely rather upon the exercise of (what you would call) their second-rate than of their first-rate qualities. As regards the education of youth, I doubt if there can be any better principle than that embodied in the well-known maxim of the Spartan king; for, after all, it is not of the highest importance that boys should become scholars, but it *is* of the highest importance that they should become *men*. And this conviction leads me to express an opinion with regard to the theory of government as having

reference to the general education of man, to which
opinion I have been brought by a consideration of
the principles of representative government as practiced in England. It appears to me that the relative
merits of representative, and arbitrary, or bureau-
cratic government are generally discussed (especially
on the Continent) within far too narrow a limit. The
great question in which the world should be interested
is, not what is the completest and strongest form of a
government, but what is the completest and grandest
form of a people. No efficiency in the mechanism of
an irresponsible government can compensate for the
absence of that active power which is only to be found
in the public life of a responsible people.

The clumsiest motion of a living body is prefera-
ble to the best-directed gesticulations of a galvanized
corpse. The English system of government begins
almost at the cradle of the Englishman, and the English
system of education continues to his grave. In this,
I think, exists the paramount excellence of both. In
England the public school, the household, the vestry-
room, the bench of magistrates, are seats of self-gov-
ernment; the polling-booth, the hustings, the House
of Commons, the Press, the Bar, are schools for self-
education. In Germany all this is wanting. Here
education stops at the University, and the intellect of
the nation is either absorbed into the pedantry of a
bureaucracy, or remains in a state of political childhood.

But I have wandered too far from the chateau at
L——. I return to my wethers.

The solitude of Edmond's childhood, his education

at home, the absence of companions of his own age, his premature intercourse with grown-up persons, gave to the boy's disposition, which was naturally thoughtful and reflective, a seriousness not common to his age. When the birth of his brother and sister, and a few years later, the entrance of Juliet into the family, introduced a more animated life into the old chateau, Edmond, who was by some years their elder, and whose character was prematurely developed, found himself, in his relations with the other children, invested with an almost paternal character.

Thus, almost from infancy, his fraternal affection for Felix and Juliet assumed a depth of earnest tenderness, a sense of protecting duty somewhat strange to the character of a child. There is nothing like that *camaraderie* which exists in the nursery. It shares all things together, tears and laughter, triumph and dismay, memory and hope. But when this loving, careless fellowship between companions in childhood is mingled with the sentiment of respect, it has in it an adoration and enthusiasm unequaled by any thing in the more conscious relations of after life. It escapes, as it were, from the little succoring hands into the earnest eyes of childhood. How proudly they smile, those trustful eyes, upon the little hero or heroine of our first adoration! How sweet it is, in our moments of early trial, to feel the gladdening glance which assures our fluttering, anxious heart that the chosen object of our emulous devotion has comprehended the struggle, and shares the triumph of some youthful effort! Schiller has beautifully indicated this sentiment in the boyish relations between Posa and Carlos.

Felix and Juliet looked up to Edmond as to a superior being. His information was extraordinary in one so young. His nature was ambitious, his understanding keen, and his enthusiasm quickly excited by whatever presented itself before him in the form of a duty.

Devotedly attached to these little ones, he could not bear the thought of their education being intrusted to strange hands. And he contrived so well to convince his father of his vocation and ability to become their teacher, that the pride of the old count was flattered by the consent which he felt himself unable to withhold from the serious charge thus enthusiastically assumed by his first-born and favorite child. This somewhat strange position which Edmond henceforth occupied between his parents and these two children seemed to result so naturally from the precocious maturity of his character, that it did not involve any apparent assumption on his part, nor any conscious weakness on the part of his father. He exerted no pressure upon those around him; they exerted no pressure upon him. Thus his rarely-gifted nature harmoniously and equably developed itself without experiencing any external restraint, but also without the inward incentive of any strong passion. Felix was passionately proud of his brother. Juliet looked up to Edmond with all the romantic ardor of an enthusiastic girl. But in this life, so free from struggle and contrariety, the weapons of the will rested unused, and the vigilant eye of mistrustful Reason closed, well pleased and self-assured, upon the peace of a happy soul.

Thus the days passed by. At last the career chosen by Felix for himself rendered necessary his entry
into a military school. The times were troubled; but
without this circumstance, family necessities and the
disposition of the boy himself would, in any case, have
decided Felix to enter the army.

This change in the customary life at L—— induced
Edmond to think of completing his own education by
travel and intercourse with the life of foreign countries. His first journey was to England. Early ini-
tiated, as he had been, into the business of country life
and the management of a great property, this country
had peculiar attractions for the young count. His
time there was not misspent. He made himself acquainted with various agricultural improvements,
which he was afterward enabled to introduce with
great advantage into the cultivation of the L—— estate. But he only came into contact with that external and superficial aspect of English life which was
most consonant to his own disposition, viz., that sort
of methodic reticence of manner which constitutes the
English notion of *Becomingness*. In England, the be-
trayal of emotion beyond a certain limit laid down by
commune consensus and general authority is, under all
circumstances, *unbecoming*. Let the heart bleed, let
the soul exult, let the breast feel ready to burst, when
all the arms of Briareus seem insufficient to clasp to
the beating heart what it yearns to embrace, and for
all this, ay, and yet more, there is, by public permission, only one set tone of voice and only one gesture
—that invariable *shake-hands*.

It was not, therefore, by his superficial and passing

intercourse with a nation which is perhaps the most earnest and impassioned in the world, that Edmond suspected even the existence of what was as yet unknown to his experience of himself—those internal hurricanes and tornadoes, which sleep perhaps unroused for years in the heart of man, but which, when once let loose, are all the more violent and destructive in proportion as the will may have neglected the foundation and enlargement of those bulwarks which are unconsciously built up by men who in early life have had to struggle with the storms of a tempestuous childhood.

Of all the wonders of London, none more fascinated the attention of the young count than that magnificent collection of objects of interest which the English need of inquiry, seeking to satisfy itself with acquisition, not only in all ages of the past, but in all parts of the world, has amassed in the metropolis within the walls of the British Museum.

The marvels of the East were then barely opened to the curiosity of the West. And here, for the first time in his life, Edmond found himself confronted with the mystic memorials of a wonderful world long since disappeared from the face of the earth, and the unintelligible but suggestive symbols of a vast and vanished epoch of human culture. His ardent desire to visit Egypt (perhaps the cradle of all our knowledge) ripened with each visit to those treasures. He commenced with zeal the preliminary studies necessary for such an enterprise.

Subsequently he went to Paris, and visited with Champollion himself the various monuments brought there by Napoleon.

Full of impatience, he set out for Marseilles, and thence embarked for the East. Well provided with letters of credit and all necessary recommendations, he reached Cairo, that *nonchalant* sentry-box before the fairy palace of the Orient which the Turks have established on the ruins of Memphis. There he hired and equipped a boat for the journey up the Nile, engaged a dragoman recommended by the English consul, and, taking with him his Herodotus, his Strabo, and a firman from Constantinople, he set forth to traverse that antique road on which the human intellect has marched for a thousand centuries, and reach the immortal ruins that yet retain the world's last traces of that Pythagorean Mind which darkly, faintly meets us in the remote and glimmering avenues of the Greek philosophy.

Various pages of the journal placed in my hands by the count indicate the interest and ardor with which he prosecuted his Oriental researches; but the scientific journal of this expedition was not confided to me with the other papers contained in the packet. Of the events of that journey only a single episode is recorded in those papers. The results of it in the subsequent life of Count Edmond were far more important than he could possibly have anticipated when this journal was written.

CHAPTER V.

A Mummy that finds means to make itself understood.

It was at Thebes.

The archæological researches of Count Edmond had brought him to that antique seat of the three last dynasties, under whose sceptre, after the expulsion of the alien conquerors, the arts and sciences of Egypt attained so vast a development, that one can not but admire as almost miraculous the destruction by Cambyses of a fabric so colossal as that of which no more than the meagre and broken outlines are revealed in the enormous magnitude of its monumental remains.

Pitching his tent from spot to spot, now amid the ruins of Luxor, now near the village of Carnac, Edmond could not reconcile himself to leave this land of marvel and of mystery till his imagination had exhausted every tangible material from which to reconstruct that hundred-gated wonder of the ancient world.

And thus, in the record now submitted to my inspection of those wandering but not unlaborious days passed by the count among the tombs, I seemed to see him, often surprised by the great sunrise of the Orient in the prosecution of his indefatigable excavations, while the bright and dewless dawn of the Desert is enlarging its noiseless light over that vast plain which, stretched broad on either side of the Nile, unites with

the Arabian range in the far East the western summits
of the Libyan hills; or else in the wide red light of hot
and windless evenings, bowed above some crumbling
byblus or papyrus, in patient solitary study, a slowly
darkened figure, silent as its shadow on the sand.

On one such evening the record shows him seated
upon the wall of that gigantic terrace which, although
builded entirely of brick, yet stands at a height of
twenty feet, and measures no less than one thousand
feet in breadth and two thousand in length.   On the
colossal pedestal, thus formed for a fabric no less enormous, stands, with its face fronting the Nile, the Temple of Ammon Chnouphis, the Divine Originative
Principle.

This immense edifice, of which the circumference
extends over a space of about three English miles, is
approached by an alley formed of six hundred colossal sphinges.   There were within it chambers vast
enough to contain the entire pile of any average-sized
mediæval cathedral; and in each chamber one hundred and thirty-four enormous columns, of which only
the ruins now remain, once supported a ceiling so
richly decorated with painting and sculpture that not
a handsbreadth of its spacious surface is bare of orna-
ment.

Beyond these stupendous structures, and well worthy of a people whose enormous works were but the
bodies of enormous thoughts, that famous lake, which,
more than a thousand years before it was witnessed
with wonder by Herodotus, had been vouchsafed by
the art of man to the need of nature, still conducts to
the Necropolis—a city of tombs and temples, whose

streets of catacombs are hewn in the solid rock of the Libyan mountains.

Over the mysterious waters of this lake to the neighboring City of the Dead had once glided (perhaps at that very hour millions of evenings ago) the ghostlike barks that bore from the dwellings of living man the bodies of the departed. Across this lake, age after age, generations upon generations had silently sailed away from the sight of the sun. And now they were all departed; and in the place that knew them no more, the only living man on whose face at that hour the sinking sunlight fell was a wanderer from lands undreamed of by the science of those starry priests who one by one had paced along that shattered pavement, and passed along that lonesome lake into the unseen world.

Amply furnished with an imperial firman and all other necessary documents, Count Edmond had previously set his numerous attendants to work upon this spot, where now, completely uncompanioned, he had withdrawn himself from his retinue, in order at his ease, and without interruption, to question the dead of secrets withheld from a thousand generations. He had just disengaged from the sheathing *byssus* in which it was preserved the mummy of a young man—perhaps a king's son.

That marvelously conservative science of the Egyptians had, in this instance, successfully disputed with time the possession of a body whose minutest atoms had for centuries been claimed in vain by the inexorable potency of corruption. The mummy was intact, perfect, complete. Stretched supine upon the sand, beneath the close and eager countenance of the German, lay the body of the young Egyptian prince, whose life had probably not numbered more than the years of the living man now breathing over him, when from that long empty husk the breath of it had departed three thousand years ago. And although in this parched and shrunken simulacrum of a human form the vital juices were withered up, yet the face of it retained upon its features the unchanged expression of the life which had once filled them. The hues and fullness, the bloom and substance of this picture of man were faded and fallen away, but the hard outline of it remained distinct and undisturbed. And as the skillful botanist instinctively recognizes in the withered flower which he examines all the once flourishing beauty of it, so Edmond, from long familiarity with those dry human specimens, had by degrees acquired a certain strange faculty of mind which enabled him, if not to bring them back to life, yet to transport himself back into the life which was once theirs, and thus, by concentrating the force and intensity of a vivid imagination, to mingle, as though he were the ghost and they the real existences, among those generations who, in times indefinitely remote, transmitted from age to age, as we to-day transmit, as others will transmit to-morrow, the warm and beating pulse of life.

According to the custom common to the Egyptians in respect to the arrangement of the dead, this mummy was accompanied by a papyrus, and this papyrus Edmond was now busily engaged in the attempt to decipher. Here in the desert, where to the student of the past the somewhat artificial atmosphere of the library and the lecture-room is replaced by the animating presence of realities and the undisturbed inspiration of Nature herself, the count had frequently succeeded, perhaps more by intuition than research, in interpreting those hieroglyphic images which, for the most part, when found in tombs or sarcophagi, represent, with little variation, the mysterious story of the migration of the soul after death, from the moment in which she leaves the body to that in which, accompanied by the two presiding genii, she stands before the solemn Balance of the Supreme Judgment. Of this mystic balance, one scale contains the Vial of Iniquity, a vase supposed to be filled with the sins of the soul, on which judgment is about to be passed, while in the opposing scale is placed a feather, an image finely conceived and of singular subtlety, representing the good actions achieved by the soul in her past existence.

Although the Babylonian rite was doubtless very different from that of the Egyptians, yet in all that regards the relations of man to the unseen powers one prevalent sentiment was so common to the various religions of Eastern antiquity—and, even in the Hebrew theosophy, so strong a substratum of Egyptian thought is to be detected—that any one who at this day peruses the strange pictures on these Egyptian papyri may not unreasonably recall the appalling pages in which the Book of Daniel records the destruction of Babylon, with a strong impression that in the interpretation given to the Babylonian king by the Hebrew seer of that unknown writing on the wall

G

there must have been an alarming significance of something more than merely *earthly* doom, and that Belshazzar may have well turned pale when the fingers of a man's hand came forth and wrote the sentence of his proved unworth, " *Thou art weighed in the balance and found wanting.*"

Between two sphinges, the symbols of wisdom, Helios and Anubis preside at the decisive ceremonial of Divine Justice. Thoth, who is easily to be recognized by the head of the Ibis, which invariably surmounts the otherwise human figure of the god, is writing the mystic record of the Soul's Trial. Before him, Harpocrates, the god of silence, is seated (somewhat uncomfortably it would appear to any but a superhuman personage) on the upper part of the crook of a divining-wand. His finger is placed upon his lips. Finally, on his throne, before the doors of the nether world, is seated the Lord and Master of All, the Divine Osiris, ready to deliver the final sentence on which are depending the future migration of the soul till the period of her purification, and the length and nature of her new probation.

But the particular papyrus which Edmond was now examining differed somewhat from the majority of these passports for Eternity. On this document a long series of images preceded the description of the soul's judgment, as though it had been sought to represent certain extraordinary scenes in the previous life of the dead man.

Between the slender figures of two youths was traced the more lofty stature of a man of mature age. This central figure was represented standing upright,

clothed with the insignia of royalty, and holding in
the right hand, which was uplifted, a ring, with which
the figure appeared to be pointing to a throne, roughly
indicated by a rude outline, in the same compartment.
Certain hieroglyphic characters, inscribed above the
heads of the three images, seemed to indicate the
names of the persons thus represented. By comparing these inscriptions with the names of the various
Pharaohs of the ancient dynasties, engraved both in
the hieroglyphic and the cursive character upon the
numerous monuments and papyri which he had already investigated, Edmond was enabled to decipher
and translate them. He could have no doubt that the
central figure of the elder personage represented the
last sovereign of the nineteenth dynasty, the Thoûoris
of Manethon, elsewhere mentioned as Rhamses, the
ninth of that name, the two other figures to the right
and left being probably (for there is no mention of
them in the historic registers) Sethos and Amasis, the
two sons of Thoûoris, who did not succeed to the
throne.

A second series of images, placed under the first
compartment, and divided from it by a border decorated by the repetition, along a horizontal ribbon, of
the initial symbol of the human figure, represented
Amasis, the younger of the two princes, inscribing various characters upon a papyrus, while at the same
time he holds uplifted in the left hand a ring, which
is no doubt the same as that which, in the first compartment, appears in the right hand of the king. In
this picture Amasis appears to be translating and inscribing on the papyrus certain characters engraved

upon the amulet of the ring. Sethos, the elder brother, with his back turned to the throne, is represented
in the act of walking away.

The third picture, divided in the same manner from
the second, shows the two brothers, each in a boat by
himself, rowing upon a stream which is doubtless that
of the Nile.

In the fourth and last group of historic figures
Sethos is alone upon the water. He is standing at
the prow of his boat with folded arms. The other
boat is upset, and a wave of the river is indicated as
passing over it. Amasis has disappeared. Only an
arm and hand, which is probably that of the drowning prince, is stretched above the surface of the water; and on the finger of that outstretched hand appears the ring which has already figured with such
apparent significance in the three preceding pictures.

From this point commences the series of images
which represents the migration of the soul of Amasis.
The soul rises from the heart of the dead in the shape
of a bird,* bearing in her beak the sacred key of the
religious mysteries. Arrived at the place of Supreme
Justice, she is presented to the tribunal by the two
plumed genii of the dead. Anubis, the messenger of
the gods, who is represented with the head of a jackal,
places beside the mystic feather, in the scale of the
soul's good actions, the ring, to which such frequent
allusion occurs in the four historic records immediately preceding this scene. Thus extraordinarily weight-

---

* This bird is a species of falcon, named in the Egyptian *Baith*,
and in other Oriental languages *Baz*. It is noteworthy that to this
day the German word for a hawking expedition is *Beize*.

ed, that scale of the mystic balance which contains the feather appears to be sinking lower than the other which contains the vial of iniquity, as though to indicate the favorable judgment of the tribunal on behalf of the soul of Amasis.*

The more than ordinary interest with which Edmond now perused the mystic annals of this somewhat perplexing papyrus was augmented by the fact that the mummy itself actually carried on the forefinger of the right hand a ring containing an amethyst of extraordinary size and beauty, on which were engraved precisely the same characters as those which Thoth was represented in the papyrus as inscribing on the records of the soul's judgment.

So profoundly was he absorbed in the minute examination of these strange and unintelligible images, that he had been utterly unconscious of the noiseless approach of a man, who, now standing beside him, with arms folded on his breast, in an attitude of intense and melancholy attention, had been for some moments past the tacit witness of the count's occupa-

---

* Nothing in these papyri representing "the Judgment after Death" is more remarkable than the frequent indication of a desire on the part of the presiding Powers to adjust the balance in favor of the good actions of the soul by some extraordinary interference. This very significantly indicates the Oriental conviction of the difficulty of reconciling, without supernatural intervention in favor of man, the aggregate shortcomings of human actions with the inexorable requirements of Supreme Justice. The conviction thus expressed, which predominates the whole of the Hebrew Scriptures from Moses to the Prophets, has no less deeply entered into the dogma of modern Christianity, which asks in fear and trembling, "Who then can be saved?" "Use every man after his deserts," says Hamlet, "and who shall 'scape whipping?"

tions. Nor was it, indeed, till the sun, now low on the western horizon, had, in its silent and stealthy prolongation of the shadows of all things, cast over the record he was perusing the dark adumbration of the stranger's tall and stately figure, that his attention was attracted toward the cause of that silent but sudden interruption.

Edmond uplifted his eyes with an amazement which was certainly not diminished by any thing in the character of the apparition upon which they rested. Draped in the massive folds of that flowing milk-white vesture which gives to its dusky wearers a dignity of form so statuesque that in their moments of motionless repose they look like antique images of mingled marble and bronze, there stood, dark eyed, dark visaged, and gazing down intensely into the startled face of the young German, one of those Kabyl chieftains whose daring raids for plunder are the terror of the travelers of the Desert.

So majestic in its immovable serenity, yet marked withal by such severity of strength in the supple grace of its sinewy stature, so suggestive of powers hostile to man, did that solitary image appear, as it stood darkly and keenly outlined against the lurid levels of the glaring west, that it might almost seem as though the silence and the solitude of the desert had suddenly heaped themselves into palpable form, and there stood in stern and sinister contemplation of their invader.

The first impulse of the count was one of self-defense. His hand made a rapid and involuntary movement toward the double-barreled rifle which was lying on the sand beside him. The Arab, without any

change of attitude or gesture, replied to this avowal
of suspicion and alarm only by a look of that inimitable contempt which is never attained but by the
features of the Orientals, and in which, whenever we
Europeans are forced to encounter it, we are conscious
of the supreme condemnation of our habitual self-
satisfaction. It is a rebuke to which there is no reply; a sentence from which there is no appeal. It
was not without a blush, of which he was painfully
conscious, that Edmond lowered his eyes abashed from
that look of tranquil scorn on the face of the Kabyl
chief.

An instant's reflection sufficed to convince him of
the ridiculous and humiliating inutility of any attempt
at self-defense; for it was sufficiently obvious that,
had any attack been intended, it might long since
have been made with the certainty of success.

"Disturb not, stranger, the repose of the tomb. It
is not well for the living to hold parley with the
dead."

It was a warning, rather than a reproach or a menace, which Edmond felt to be conveyed to him by
these words, abruptly uttered in that *lingua franca*
which, throughout the Orient, forms a neutral ground
of language whereon the various races of the East
and West may encounter each other upon equal terms.

Pleased with any pretext for escape from his previous embarrassment, and well content to find one in
the common resources of conversation, the count hastened to reply to this sudden appeal.

"You might say well," he answered, "if this tomb
were less taciturn than I have found it. It obstinately

refuses, however, to answer my question. And yet I have not sought from it any secret of the other world. I simply ask it to restore to this life what from this life it has robbed."

"Fool!" said the Arab; "and who hath told thee it is good for the living that the tomb should restore to their knowledge the secrets it is bidden to withhold? Knowest thou aught of the nature of any force, and whether it be of good or of evil, so long as that force is hidden, and the action of it laid to sleep?"

"Certainly," murmured Edmond, half to himself, "I know not of any force of which I can conceive that it should retain the faculties of action after a slumber so immeasurably prolonged."

The stranger did not immediately reply. A profound melancholy seemed to darken in the intricate depths of the luminous eye which he fixed upon the count as he slowly answered, after a momentary silence,

"Say you so? Yet a grain of corn, taken from the tomb to-day, and cast into the furrow to-morrow, will grow from the blade cut down by the sickle that reaped in the harvests of the Pharaohs ere the glory of these was gathered into the garners of Time. And can you doubt of the immortality of forces far mightier than those that germinate in the grain of corn which you take from the tomb where they slumber, or suppose that the centuries, survived by the seed of the field, can annihilate the seed of the soul?"

Edmond was no less struck by the peculiar tone of voice with which these words were uttered than by the accuracy of the illustration they suggested; for he had frequently convinced himself of the fact that corn found deposited with mummies in symbol of sacrifice perfectly retains its faculty of germination.

"After all, though," he replied, "if I must grant you the existence of the fact to which you allude, yet I confess that I can think of nothing except a blade of corn from which this sort of palingenesis can be expected."

The Arab approached the mummy that was lying on the sand before the count. He stood over the wizened corpse for some time in profound silence. The ardent and intense regard of those dark and intricate eyes was plunged in piercing scrutiny upon the withered features of the dead man's brown, adust, and stolid face. Not a muscle was moved on the cheek of the Kabyl. Under the lustrous transparency peculiar to the complexion of Orientals, nothing agitated the stern metallic reflection of the firm bronzen features, not less brown nor less immovable than those of the mummy at his feet. But ever and anon from beneath the mysterious languors and soft depth of shadow with which the long, slumbrous eyelash veiled the vigilant eye, Edmond could notice, not without an emotion far from comfortable, that strange lights and flashes, as though struck out from some fierce agony of soul, were passing and darting in lurid, sinister play.

Suddenly at length the Arab stretched forth his swarthy arm, and seized the dead man's hand. He drew the ring from its withered finger, and fixed his glittering eye upon the purple, luminous stone, intently perusing the characters engraved upon it.

"Yes," he muttered, as though continuing aloud

G 2

some dialogue commenced within himself, "Behold the fateful words of Seb Kronos, the Indestructible Destroyer! .... MINE IS THE WORLD, AND TO ME MUST ALL THINGS COME. I, SOLE, HAVE CREATED; AND I, SOLE, DESTROY. I WILL WHAT I WILL. I GIVE AND I TAKE AWAY. ON MORTALS I BESTOW, AND FROM MORTALS I WITHHOLD, HAPPINESS. MAN, THAT ART MADE OF THE DUST OF THE EARTH, DISTURB NOT THE HAND OF DESTINY. TOUCH NOT WITH EARTHLY FINGER THE WORK OF FATE."

"Tell me," exclaimed Edmond, "is that indeed the sense of the amulet?"

"It is the *words* of the amulet," said the other, and he passed the ring into the hands of the count. "Blessed thou," he added, after a pause, "if thou never ascertain the sense of them. He that first discovered the significance of those words lies stretched before thee. Behold the first victim of the oracle!"

The Arab pointed to the mummy at his feet. Then taking the papyrus from the hand of Edmond, "Lo, here," he said, "Thoûoris and his sons; Sethos the elder, Amasis the younger.

"Ignoring the prerogative of birthright, the king areads the monarchy to him that shall read the riddle of the ring, as being the most wise and worthiest to reign. Verily not wise was he that thus reversed the rule of Nature. Now, of the sons of Thoûoris, the most wise was Amasis; forasmuch as in him was an excellent spirit of knowledge, to understand the writings of the gods, and in the showing forth of hard sentences. He, therefore, to his hurt, resolved the riddle of the ring.

"DISTURB NOT THE HAND OF DESTINY.

"TOUCH NOT WITH EARTHLY FINGER THE WORK
OF FATE.

"So Amasis read the writing, and declared the interpretation thereof. Deeply within his inmost heart Sethos kept those words. Even as they were graven upon the stone of the ring, so also were they graven upon the spirit of the man.

"And from him the Most High God removed the kingdom and the glory of it, so that the sceptre departed out of the hand of Sethos and was given to his brother, that he should sit on the throne of his fathers after the death of Thoûoris the king.

"Then Sethos bowed his head, and was obedient to the will of the Most High God, revering the words of the Oracle.

"But neither did he forget those words in the after time. Therefore he lifted not his hand, neither in anywise hindered he the work of the Inevitable, when to him his brother (was it not by the fault of the man himself? and was it not by the will of the Most High?), being in evil case, a drowning man without help, stretched forth from out of the whelming of the waters a suppliant hand.

"And so Amasis perished under the eye of his brother Sethos. For the waters took him, and he died."

"And what became of Sethos?" exclaimed Edmond, whose imagination was stretched to the utmost by the strange recital which thus suddenly illuminated the hitherto unelucidated obscurity of that antique tragedy imaged on the papyrus which he had in vain been attempting to decipher.

A bitter smile played about the hard-lined angles of the lips of the Kabyl chief.

"Saidst thou not thyself," he answered (and a look of inexpressible mockery accompanied these words, slowly and emphatically pronounced), "saidst thou not thyself that thou seekest not from the tomb the secrets of another world?"

· Edmond, again overmastered by the supreme mockery which he felt in the tone of this response, was compelled to lower his eyes from the face of the Kabyl. They rested on the gem which he yet held in his hand. The mystic amethyst seemed to dart at him from the glittering and vindictive angles of its luminous facets violet forked fires and flashes of unholy light.

Meanwhile the sun had sunk unnoticed behind the dark summits of the Libyan mountains. And now the large disk of the full moon was swathing in soft, argent light the hot, transparent air, and sultry spaces of the great solitude. When the count again lifted up his eyes, he perceived that the mysterious inhabitant of that solitude had left his side as noiselessly as he had approached it. He could distinctly trace the tall form of the Desert's dusky son silently gliding into darkness among the mighty trunks of the colossal columns of the temple of Ammon Chnouphis.

CHAPTER VI.

DOUBTS.

ALL search after the Arab chief proved fruitless. The attendants of Edmond, whom he had left about the encampment at some little distance from the scene of his strange interview with the Kabyl, had noticed neither the approach nor the departure of that mysterious visitant. On the morrow careful inquiries were instituted by order of the count throughout the surrounding villages. Without result, however. Far and wide, for many weeks past, no trace had been seen, no news had been heard, of any Kabyl troop. Those formidable marauders had been probably kept at a respectful distance by the numerous and well-armed escort of Count R——.

His interview with the Arab appeared more and more mysterious the more he considered it. No third person had been present on the spot, or even within sight of the speakers. The monuments and the dead were witnesses that could not be called into court. To increase his perplexity. Nature herself seemed to have entered into conspiracy with Circumstance, by refusing all testimony to the fact. The fine, smooth sand which overlies those ruins showed nowhere, either on the spot where the Kabyl had been standing, or along those places over which he must have passed when he disappeared into the temple of Ammon Chnouphis, the trace of any footsteps which could reasonably be attributed to him. Had the night wind, itself a phantom, jealous of any other spectral presence on its own domain, been careful to cancel before dawn all record of that apparition? Anyhow, no proof of the supposed interview could be educed from the count's knowledge of the story of Amasis. The images on the papyrus were sufficiently unusual to have stimulated his imagination, and sufficiently suggestive of such a story to have enabled him to construct it unconsciously from the supplementary materials of his own fancy. There rested the interpretation of the ring. But what proved that interpretation to be the right one? Those characters, even according to the hypothesis of which he could not feel quite sure that he was not the unconscious author, must have been enigmatical to the science of the Egyptians themselves. Nay, even the amethyst was a stone not common (perhaps unknown) to that people. Every thing in the character of the story seemed to indicate a theology anterior even to that of Egypt. But how, then, did the ring come into the count's hand? Had he himself drawn it from the finger of the mummy? If so, why had he no recollection of that act? Was it possible that, in the act of possessing himself of the ring, the consciousness of the action, which had a *real* existence, had been, as it were, submerged and obliterated in the superimposed consciousness of something which had only an *ideal* existence?

Whichever way he turned it, the mystery remained. Finally, he accustomed himself to look back at it through the *chiar' oscuro* of doubt; and, thus viewed, amid many conflicting and equally unsatisfactory conjectures, the supposition that the whole occurrence had been a sort of waking dream (the effects of watching and the distemperature of an overlabored brain), although not entirely nor permanently accepted by the count (for what man in possession of his senses will willingly reject their evidence?), yet, on the whole, assumed the most prominent and the most durable place in his mind. Thus, in proportion as the mysterious image of the Arab was driven from the domain of external fact, and ceased to represent *a reality*, retreating into the recesses of internal consciousness, imperceptibly it assumed possession of *an idea*.

An idea which I can only indicate by this question:

With the bodily eye Edmond had not looked on the face of the Kabyl chief? Perhaps. But had his spiritual eye been resting on the soul of Sethos the Egyptian?

A fanciful inquiry this, which I seize as it rises in my own mind, and throw out at random.

CHAPTER VII.

WESTWARD HO!

THE approach of that season which is the most important of all to the inhabitants of Egypt, who still take for the bases of their calendar those three phenomena of the Egyptian year, the overflow of the Nile, the maturity of crops, and the season of dryness, now barely left time to Count Edmond, before the rising of the waters, to regain Cairo, the starting-point of his expedition.

There, having safely confided to the care of trustworthy agents, to be shipped for Europe, the rich result of his recent researches, he set out without farther delay upon his homeward journey.

And here the golden-gated Orient fades out of the foreground of this narrow stage, whereon is to be rehearsed the tragedy of a life; fades, dream-like, into Dream; yet in the far background still, incongruous and strange, some faintest ghostly shadow of its "gorgeous palaces, its solemn temples," may haply linger, even as the memory of a dream will sometimes linger, out of place, amid the business of waking life, leaving, of all its "insubstantial pageant," yet "a wrack behind."

If we are, indeed, no more than "such stuff as dreams are made of," what function, amid the brief activities of this "little life" that is "rounded with a sleep," may the Maker of it have assigned to the memory of a dream?

BOOK II.

𝔗𝔥𝔢 𝔖𝔬𝔴𝔦𝔫𝔤 𝔬𝔣 𝔱𝔥𝔢 𝔖𝔢𝔢𝔡.

Our acts our angels are, or good or ill,
The haunting shadows that walk by us still.

FORD.

BOOK II.

CHAPTER I.

THE EGYPTIAN GALLERY AT L——.

WITH those pages which conclude the account of his Egyptian journey, and of which the substance has been recorded in the preceding chapters of the present narrative, the journal of Count Edmond breaks off. It is resumed again at a later date, from which I gather that between the period of the count's return from the East and that at which the journal recommences about a year and a half must have elapsed; and I assume from the silence of the journal in respect of this intervening period, either that the writer of it was during that time too busily occupied to record the daily events of his life, or that those events were of a nature too trivial and insignificant to be recorded.

The first page of the second portion of the journal is dated from the old chateau of the count's father in Silesia. Here Edmond appears to be, as formerly, the idol of the household, and the central figure in the family picture, which, but for the absence of his brother Felix, who, it appears, is still at the Military College, would seem to be complete. The various details of family matters, and the quiet chronicles of country life, which occupy the early pages of this part of the journal, I see no need to recapitulate; and I

shall therefore resume my own recital of this strange
history of a life, which I have herein undertaken to
set forth, by bringing at once before the reader the first
scene which arrested my attention in the perusal of
those pages with which the count's narrative recommences. This scene is the first distinct indication I
can find of a new phase in the fraternal character of
the relations between Edmond and Juliet, and perhaps a new phase in the two characters themselves.

Few, I think, who, after long absence, have been
restored to the sight of those they love, will have failed to experience in the first moment of reunion an indescribable sensation, of which the peculiar charm is
probably produced by the mysterious commixture in
a single influence, or in two that are simultaneous, of
that which is familiar with that which is strange.
These apparitions are in one and the same moment
altogether old and altogether new; the same and yet
changed; they soothe, and yet surprise us. Perhaps
this complex sensation is never so strongly or so
strangely felt as when absence has removed from our
sight the silent and delicate stages of that tender,
flower-like change by which childhood passes into
womanhood, and we breathe with a delicious embarrassment the thrilling and unwonted atmosphere of a
new and yet well-known presence in that magic moment which for the first time mingles to sight and
sense the ghost of the child we left with the vision of
the woman that meets us.

With the happiest emotions of that moment of reunion there mingles a vague, half-conscious sadness.
This sense of melancholy has its secret source in the

imperfect apprehension of some indefinite change in
the nature of a happiness which has been a habit of
the heart—a happiness of which the permanency has
hitherto seemed sufficiently insured by the invariable
tranquillity of its character. At that boundary-line
before which our accustomed sensations pause abashed
and uncertain of themselves, the charming uncon-
sciousness of the child is mingled with the charm of
the coming consciousness of the woman—never more
charming than in that first moment when she herself
is just beginning to apprehend the new nature of her
own womanhood. The future and the past—the being that was and the being that will be—hover in a
holy twilight over the heaven of that brief time wherein the insubstantial present is but an airy apparition,
haunting and beautifying the atmosphere in which
memory melts into anticipation, purifying and sub-
limating the sense by which the presence of it is apprehended, and hallowing the heart into which the
sanctity of it is received.·

I have never yet met with a man whose nature,
however churlish, callous, or uncultured, has not been,
in some part of it, susceptible to this sanctifying influence when confronted with the presence of that
mystery of beauty which is unveiled by the first hours
of virgin womanhood. We approach it with a deference such as royalty does not receive from the sleek-
est of its courtiers; and even when it manifests itself
only in that embarrassment which is the feeblest expression of it, it is graced in our behaviors by a certain sacred shyness.

The degree to which Edmond was susceptible to

this influence is apparent in numberless allusions throughout those parts of his journal which I have not thought it necessary to transcribe. His susceptibility to such influences must, indeed, have been proportioned to the extreme tenacity of self-seclusion and reserve which had become the habit of his mind. Within that mind thus habitually locked fast, and as it were impenetrably shut within itself, there existed depths and breadths of a vast mine of undivulged value, of which the multitudinous galleries had not yet been obstructed or choked up by any internal convulsion. Thus the new sentiment all at once, and once for all, entered at every aperture of his consciousness; penetrated, unimpeded, all those empty galleries; filled full the hollow void; sunk down from depths to deepest depths; and illumined with a soft, loving light the inmost recesses of his heart. All things became in him, as in a church, silent and holy. When he spoke with her whom he could no longer call sister, his voice grew softer and deeper. When he was with others in her presence, little that he ever said was spoken *to* her; all that he ever said was spoken *for* her.

In short, there was a change in Edmond. It was the change of his feeling for Juliet. Juliet herself was changed. And if there was no change in her feeling for Edmond, the expression of that feeling was at least no longer the same. For her, Edmond had ever been the complete and quintessential embodiment of all that is good and noble. What in others she had found to admire more rarely, and in less degree, was realized to the full perfection in the faultless impression of his character upon hers. It was mentally and morally, no less than actually, that in childhood she had looked up to him; and as childhood expanded and deepened into womanhood, and the horizon of her nature enlarged its scope, she still found in the mind of Edmond the same distance and the same height, and still looked up to him with the same wondering, trustful gaze. Thus the growth of her nature had changed nothing in the relations of it to his; for her power to ask still fell short of his power to give, and the same surpassing proportions still returned the lavish response to the larger need.

It was the critical, the decisive moment in which it had become possible for the lives of these two beings to commingle and amalgamate into one; nay, in which it was certain that they must indissolubly so amalgamate, if only the deeper and more thoughtful feeling with which, in the dawn of her new self-consciousness, Juliet now regarded Edmond, should be met and seized at the outset by the merest impulsion on his part, and so imperceptibly turned into the direction which a woman's feelings, in that moment of her life when they are first discovered by herself, take all at once and once for all, at the lightest touch of a loving hand.

But the moment slipped away. Passion only knows how to strike the want into the will, and grasp the intention in the act; for passion only, knowing well and surely what it wants, stretches out the hand to take it: in rude natures, rashly, without thought; in strong natures, instinctively, without thinking.

Edmond was devoid of passion. Contemplating its

own sensations, this nature soared and hovered, as it were, with outstretched wings over its proper consciousness, in a region of passionless perception, attracting into itself the outer world, and there transforming actual objects into ideal images, instead of boldly passing out of itself into the world of external things, and there firmly planting the foot of conquest on the ground of possession. Thus to him, his sensations about facts *were* facts. He thought to pass his life forever with Juliet. He could contemplate no other circumstantial possibility. This thought was firmly established in him. It remained a thought. The process of thinking it once completed, nothing else presented itself to his mind as necessary and natural to the realization of it. The farther process of acting it out did not occur to him—to him the thought was an action. The matter was fully and finally settled in his mind, and so in his mind it remained. It was a virgin sentiment in a virgin nature which realizes possession in the reality of the feeling by which it is possessed. Thus the days passed tranquilly and happily away.

The long-delayed arrival of Edmond's Egyptian wonders, however, was a great event at the chateau. Unheard-of preparations had been made for the reception of these venerable visitors. Half the house had been turned topsy-turvy on their account. To assimilate the aspect of the new museum to that of the marvels it was destined to contain, some of the old mediæval chambers had been duly Egyptianized. The Gothic fireplaces, furnished after much difficulty by the village mason with an adequate quantity of py-

lones and capitals, gradually contrived to assume as
sepulchral and forbidding an appearance as could possibly be desired, and finally looked as proud of themselves as if the only ashes they had ever contained
were those of Osiris himself.

The workmen had bivouacked in the best rooms,
and kept up a series of light skirmishes about the rest
of the house for several months; so that, when at last
the arrival of the gods was announced, all was in readiness for their reception with due honor and dignity.

It was some time before the untraveled members
of the household felt themselves to be on quite friendly terms with the mummies. But the beautiful serious sphinges, with their smooth lion-limbs, and serene
human faces, immediately made themselves perfectly
at home. Speedy popularity, too, was acquired by
the placid divinities themselves, with their quiet, astonished, childish faces, notwithstanding their very distressing habit of permanently keeping one leg raised
at an angle of thirty degrees above the ground, apparently with no object but to make one feel uncomfortable in trying to realize the extent of discomfort suggested by such a position. Their neat priestly head-
dresses (worn to this day in Egypt), and their quiet
behavior, and sleek, lustrous limbs of polished granite,
did much, moreover, to mollify in their favor the instinctive repugnance for "pagan idols, and outlandish,
heathenish images," with which the uncritical menial
mind was disposed at first to regard these chaste
embodiments of the speculative thought of Ancient
Egypt. Every body cheerfully lent a helping hand
to the arrangement of the museum, which soon pre-

H

sented a very respectable arrangement of gems, scara-
bæi, sphinges, stuffed crocodiles, and tupinambes, sarcophagi, statues, papyri, pedestals, plinths, capitals,
gods, and columns.

"Oh beautiful! what a magnificent ring!"

It is Juliet that makes this exclamation. She is
helping Edmond, as usual, this afternoon to assort
and arrange sundry little odds and ends of antiquity
that are still to be put in order. She takes the ring
from its little cotton bed in the case where she has
just found it; holds it up, and turns about the stone
(a beautiful purple amethyst) in the warm light that is
streaming in, and beaming on her bright young face
through the high window of the Egyptian Gallery.

Edmond is busily occupied in stretching out a papyrus, which appears to be in an advanced state of de-
composition. He is not paying much attention to
Juliet just now, so he answers without turning his
head. "What! have you really found, after all, something that pleases you among these uncannie curiosities? How glad I am!"

"Thanks, Edmond! It is perfect. Suits me exactly. I suspect you must have had it made expressly for me by one of the goldsmiths of Serastro."

So says Juliet, her ideas about matters Egyptian not
ranging beyond sundry confused recollections of the
libretto of the Zauberflöte.

"See how it fits my finger!" and she spreads out
her five slender little fingers to be looked at, and suns
her soft white hand in the warm light.

"Charming! Now don't suppose that you are ever to regain possession of this ring. It is mine, do you understand? forever and ever. *Par droit de conquête et par droit de naissance.* Do you hear? for it certainly must have been made for me, or I for it. See! And I intend never to yield it but with my life. *Gare aux voleurs!*

But Edmond is still too busy with his papyrus to turn round and admire the rosy, impudent little finger that is shaking defiance at all the divinities of the Nile.

"Ah! Juliet, Juliet, boast not too loud, or at least too soon. (Another woful rent in this poor papyrus. Sad!) If you will not yield the ring but with your life, then must you give it to whoever shall one day be the possessor of that same dear life of yours; and may he take good care of both the precious gifts!"

"So be it!" she answers, laughing. "And it shall be my spousal ring. This and no other. I am sure, too, it will bring me good luck. 'Tis doubtless an amulet or a talisman. See the wonderful characters here on the stone! Some mighty meaning they must have, no doubt. One fancies how some old wizard must have puzzled his own wise head how best to puzzle all the foolish heads in the world with this posy, for years and years, till at last he turned himself into a stone, like your friends Horus and Anubis, and what other spider-legged gods you may please to teach me the unpronounceable names of."

So saying and so laughing, she comes up to Edmond, stooping all the fragrance of her soft brown hair over that unsavory papyrus which he has just succeeded in lodging safely under its glass frame.

So this time Edmond turns round, and . . . .
ah! that ever-recurring note of the hautboy in my
ears! . . . . there comes over him, all at once,
a sort of cold, creepy shudder, and that strangely-
common feeling in the hair, as if damp fingers of an
unseen hand were passing through the roots of it from
behind.   Nor, though I fancy him to be standing full
in the sunshine of Juliet's laughing eyes, am I, on the
whole, I must confess, disposed to wonder very much
at this uncomfortable feeling which he describes himself to have felt just then, for the ring which he sees
on the finger of Juliet is the antique ring of Seb Kronos, which he had first seen on the finger of Amasis
of Thebes.

Instantaneously, as at the touch of a wizard's wand,
all his senses are transported back amid the imme-
morial ruins of the temple of Ammon Chnouphis.
He sees and hears the irrevocable rolling of the ancient Nile.   Out from the whelming wave, upstretched
as though to him, in agonizing effort, he sees the arm
and hand of Amasis.   Alone on the prow of his boat,
standing unmoved, immovable, he sees Sethos the
Egyptian.   And the features of the face of Sethos are
the features of the face of the Kabyl chief.   He feels
fixed keenly on his own the venomous eye of the
Arab.   Out from the incandescent heart of the kindling amethyst begin to dartle and to flash violet rays
of lurid fire; and the fiery rays fiercely writhe and
twist, and weave themselves up into the empty air
before his eyes into angry letters of a luminous, bewildering writing.   Forthwith come faint and far-off
sounds, as though out of illimitable distance; and the

sounds enter, like wicked souls, into the violet flame-bodies of the lurid letters of the written words, so that the words begin to mutter and to speak to him; and he hears the voices of the words as a man hears voices in a dream, which make a sound that is like a silence. And the sentence of the words that are uttered by the flame is the sentence of the words of Seb Kronos, the Indestructible Destroyer: "To MORTALS I GIVE, AND FROM MORTALS I TAKE, HAPPINESS. DISTURB NOT THE HAND OF DESTINY!"

"Well, whenever you have finished your profound perusal of my talisman, I shall expect you, Edmond, to satisfy my curiosity with the interpretation of the hieroglyphics."

It is the voice of Juliet beside him. This sweet voice shatters the weird spell, and recalls him at once within the sphere of that gentle presence, whose sunny serenity is incapable of being troubled by any wizardry more wicked than perhaps the pert pranks of some playful Puck. Immediately all the magic was melted out of the ring; and Edmond, ashamed of his own unaccountable, but merely momentary disturbance of mind, was just about to explain to Juliet that he had in vain attempted to decipher the hieroglyphics, when, suddenly and blithely, in the great court-yard outside, sound the shrill, clear notes of a postillion's horn. It was no doubt the distant notes of this horn which, a few moments ago, had lent their phantom echoes to the fancied language of the fiery letters, in that rapid vision which had rushed for but an instant across the mind of Edmond. And thus a jolly German post-boy, blowing his horn, as he bumped along, in leather

breeches, on his way to the chateau, had unconsciously
been enacting, in the imaginary drama of another
man's mind, no less solemn and important a part than
that of the divine Seb Kronos.

Immediately afterward a post-chaise rolls rumbling
into the court, beneath the window where Edmond is
standing with Juliet. A light elastic step in rapid
movement on the stair; confused voices along the cor-
ridor; nearer and clearer; the door is dashed open;
wherethrough also comes dashing at full speed, with
a mighty clatter of spurs and sabre, into the Egyptian
Gallery, quite regardless of

"Osiris, Apis, Orus, and their crew,"

a blooming young officer; and Felix, with a light, joyous laugh, flings himself into the arms of Edmond.

CHAPTER II.

FELIX.

THIS was the first meeting of the brothers since Edmond's return. When Edmond came home from his Egyptian journey, Felix was still at the military school at M——. Soon after his arrival at L——, Edmond wrote from the chateau to Felix, proposing to visit him at M—— in case his brother should be unable to obtain leave of absence. To this proposal Felix replied speedily and privately by the following letter, which I select from the numerous papers made over to me by the count, and copy without alteration or abridgment, as a tolerably fair specimen of the difference of character between the two brothers.

FELIX TO EDMOND.

M——. Marked *Private and Confidential.*

Undated.

"Brother, don't come! Keep my secret; but, for God's sake, *don't come.* Fancy me crammed up to my ears for examination; loaded up to the muzzle (do you understand?) and ready to go off. I mean to take the dear old gentlefolks at home by surprise, and so I am going up a month before term. I can't hold out any longer. I can't live on in this way, separated from all of you. I can't bear it, I say. And so, heighho! there is no help for it but to work, work, work (and oh! if you knew how I hate working!), day and night, night and day, at square root and cube, cube root and square, till I am fairly in the way to reduce myself to a decimal fraction. Now, shouldst thou come here, and were I to see thee, thou best and dearest of men, it would be all up with the curves and hyperboles. For, as for the mathematics, know that I am a dunce among the dunces. 'Oh dear Horatio, I am ill at these matters,' and what between *plus* here and *minus* there, hang it! the game lies so close, and the cover is so thick, that I am always making a false point of it, in despite of all thy teaching and training, oh thou inimitable Euclid! No! by St. Hubert I swear it, till all is fairly over, I will hear and think of nothing but the *emth root* of *m* (mark this!) *plus n*, to the power of *s*, *plus m minus n* to the power of *r minus m plus n minus q* to the power of *t plus* the *emth root* of *r*, divided by *m plus n plus p plus q plus r plus x y z botherorum* . . . . *Ouf! Bacchus, Apollo, divorum!*

"Brandy and Seltzer-water! and find me the *enth root* of it all, if you can. My head whirls, Edmond, when I think how I might be hugging you all to my heart of hearts just now, instead of splitting these dull brains of mine on all the tormenting angles of trigonometry! To say nothing of these lamentable logarithms! Well, well! thank Heaven, it only wants eighty-seven days now to Easter! Eighty-seven days at twenty-four hours *per diem*, minus six hours' sleep ('tis the least I can do with), equals two thousand and eighty-eight hours minus five hundred and twenty-two hours; equals fifteen hundred and sixty-six hours. Minus again twenty-five minutes one and a quarter seconds *per diem* for breakfast, dinner, *et cœtera*, remains fifteen hundred and twenty-two hours. Then there is still minus two hours *per diem* riding—(oh! you should see the old roan now! I have her down here, in first-rate condition)—that makes one thousand four hundred and sixteen hours' work. And in this space of time must I mark, learn, and inwardly digest. Differential Calculus. Faith! 'tis enough to make a man mount on a Flutter-mine, and blow out his brains, the sooner to get rid of all the stuff he has got into them. No matter, though! All is going on well. I shall manage to swallow the whole dose, I think. I am not afraid of the drugs, least of all of the *Military History* part of the emetic. Let them only ask me who gained the battle of Preston Pans, and if I answer Frederick the Great, I should like to see the König-licher Preussischer Professor who will venture to pluck me. Humph!

"Brother, brother, not a word of all this! Ear of my heart as thou art, be silent—silent as the tombs of Nineveh. Where is Nineveh, by the way? I hope they'll not ask me that. I suspect it must be in Pomerania: five hundred inhabitants; one thousand seven hundred houses; one Protestant chapel; ditto three Moravian; eight synagogues; two porcelain manufactories; and—if that's not right, the devil take the geographers for putting it into my head!

"Oh Edmond! Edmond! if you did but know what goes on in this head of mine! Is it not a shame to

H 2

think how many things have taken place in the world which I, poor devil! must needs know something about now ?"

" 'Tis enough, oh brother mine, to put me in envy of the good old times of Cain and Abel. Lucky dogs, those brothers! Nothing had then happened to trouble men's heads but a damned apple. Easy enough in those days to pass one's examination. And if only that silly fellow Cain—fool! not to know the worth of his own good luck! why must he needs . . . . . But 'tis I am the fool, brother Edmond. Dolt! how came this nonsense into my head? I to be prating of Cain—such a fellow as Cain, forsooth!—I, who am writing to Edmond—Edmond, my prince of good fellows—the best of brothers and dearest of men!

" Ay, and believe it, brother—for, trust me, this is as true and sure as that the sine of the angle is equal to the cosines multiplied by the tangent of it, or no matter in whatsoever other formula thou mayest be graciously pleased to receive the assurance—to no man on earth is Edmond half so dearly dear as to his stupid, good for nothing, but faithful and ever loving

" FELIX."

Edmond faithfully kept his brother's secret. He wrote to Felix two or three times a week, to encourage him. But he had not expected him home so soon.

For I find, by reference to the dates of the papers in my hands, that the day on which this event occurred was the 21st of March, 1813.

So, after the first joyous greetings were over, Edmond drew his brother aside.

"How about the examination?" he whispers to Felix. "Can I speak out about it now? Are we to
congratulate you?"

Whereupon Master Felix bursts into an immoder-
ate fit of laughter; and, turning round to the others,

"Oh, ay! the examination?" says he. "A famous
farce, and you shall hear all about it.

"Passed my examination, have I, do you ask? I
should think I *have* passed it, indeed! And what sort
of an examination, too? That is the best of the joke.
Faith! brother Edmond, I verily believe that the
Seven Sages of Greece, and yourself into the bargain,
had you all been present on that auspicious occasion,
would have held your sides for laughing.

"But no matter. The thing is done. This time,
as luck would have it, it was not I, but the professors
themselves that were at pains to pull me through.
Never yet, you may be sure, was the Ass's Bridge
made so smooth to the hoof of the ass; for, be it here-
by known to all whom it may concern, that it was settled beforehand in the council of the gods that I should
be, with the utmost expedition compatible with the
constitution of the Prussian mind, an officer in His
Majesty's Army. The great Napoleon absolutely insisted on it.

"Why are you all staring at me in that way? Do
none of you know, here in your corner, what the
whole world is about outside?

"Our King has appealed to the people!

"No more University, no more Lyceum, no more
Military Colleges, no more Government Offices! Student and schoolboy, cadet and clerk—in short, every

man that can bear arms, is turned soldier! Hurrah!
the French garrison has walked itself off—bolted—
cut its sticks!

"When I left Berlin on the 17th, York, the fine old
York, entered the town at the head of seventeen thousand picked troops. You should have seen the rejoic-
ing there was that day.

"Yesterday I presented myself before Lutzow at
Breslau; enrolled myself the same day in his Free
corps; and, what is more, Edmond, you are my com-
rade and fellow-officer; for your commission, old fellow, is signed, sealed, and packed up in my portmanteau.

"What say you? I and you, *cum canibus nostris*—
all our dogs—are after the Bonaparte. The old fox
has broken cover, and there is nothing but tallyho!
after the heels of him from one end of the land to the
other. What fun!

"To-day and to-morrow are still ours to make the
most of, mother. After to-morrow I promised Lutzow
that we would both appear under arms."

*   *   *   *   *   *   *

The political events in Europe which followed the
scene witnessed by Felix on the 17th of March, 1813,
are well known.

Merged in the current of these public events, the
private history of the two brothers entirely passes
out of sight till the signature of the Treaty of Paris,
which enabled them, with the rest of their comrades
in arms, to return home.

The following letters and papers, carefully selected from the great mass of private documents confided to my care by Count R——, are sufficient to give consistency and continuity to the development of his extraordinary and melancholy biography.

CHAPTER III.

JULIET.

JULIET TO THERESA.

L——, 14th June, 1814.

"AH! what a day, dear Theresa! Edmond and Felix are both come home. My dear, good, darling brothers! Both of them well, both of them the same as in the pleasant old times, and yet . . . . . Well, let me tell you how it has all happened.

"I was sitting in the window that overlooks the park. Our dear mother was sitting a little way off at her work-table. You remember (do you not?) this sunny little study of ours, where you used to share with me my solitude, in the days when Edmond was first away on his journey in Egypt. And have you forgotten that long summer, when you and I managed to coax three or four of the tallest vine-boughs up the espaliers on the wall, and in through the casement, so as to make for us two girls to be queens of, sole and undisputed, a little green bower in the room itself. The bower has grown since then, Theresa. And here, where I sit behind the leaves and twigs, my small green palace walls are as closely and compactly framed and clothed as the nest of the noisy swallow up yonder in the eaves outside. How sure I felt this spring that the swallow's news was good!

"We had just received letters from Strasbourg

which made us expect their return, but not so soon, for they had not then received their *congé.*

"Well, as I am sitting here, all at once I hear a noise in the espaliers under the window. Crack, crack! crash, crash! and before I can turn my head to see what is the matter, lo and behold! a saucy young gentleman in uniform climbs over the window, jumps into the room, whisks me out of my chair, catches me up in his right arm as if I were a feather, pulls me, or rather carries me, in this way across the room, and, seizing mother after the same unceremonious fashion with his other arm, squeezes and kisses us both out of breath; while the dear old lady, really, I think, speechless from pure joy, can only strain his beaming, sunburnt face to her bosom, and stroke her hand over his tossed and tumbled curls without uttering a word.

"We had hardly recovered from our first happy bewilderment at the unexpected appearance and frantic impetuosity of Felix (for of course it was he; who but Felix would have ever dreamed of jumping in at the window?) when Edmond also came in through the door, holding father by the hand. Oh, then, Theresa, 'twas nothing but kissing and clasping all round, hands in hands and hearts to hearts! Felix laughed and cried in one and the same breath, and jumped about like mad. When at last he had kissed and hugged us all round for at least the fiftieth time, then he began to seize his brother by the head, and dance round him, shouting and singing, and hugging him too, as if they also now met for the first time after a year's absence. *Bref.* he finally played so many pranks with

us all, that we soon fairly laughed off all the trouble
and trepidation of those first breathless moments of
sudden joy.

* * * * * * * *

"At last the Kobold is tamed. He is fast asleep
now in his mother's chair, where all at once his eyelids dropped. I think the French cannon would not
wake him just now; and I hope he will leave us all
in repose for a while.

"Edmond staid with us longer. He who appeared
so calm and self-possessed on his arrival, has, however, been deeply agitated, I now suspect, by the meeting. We were obliged to force him to take a little
rest; for the poor boys have been nine days on the
road, Theresa, without stopping night or day. And
they came home on a wretched peasant's cart, for the
post communications are not yet quite re-established.
My dear, dear brother! while I write to you, Theresa,
and while Felix is snoring loud enough to break the
drum of my ears, I can see Edmond wandering about
all alone in the park instead of taking any rest. I
hoped he was in bed long ago and asleep by this time.

"There he is now (I can see him through the window), standing near my little garden. I think I must
have told you how I planted there a large E and a
large F in box. The F looks fresher and thicker, and
greener and stronger than the E. It has grown so.
I am sorry. But it is from no want of care or coax-
ing on my part. I could not help it. There is one
part of the earth where the box has withered down as
often as I planted it. What a strange nature is Edmond's! So dreamy and quiet; yet he notices every

thing. Nothing escapes his eye. So it always was
with him. And he often attaches to the merest trifles
a greater value than to things which are really important. I have many times observed that. Would
you think it, Theresa? Soon after he first came into
the room, he had already noticed, from my window,
the withered side of the box E in my garden. I saw
him looking at it. As for Felix, that saucy, misbe-
haved urchin has never even vouchsafed me a Thank-
you for all my care and pains. It is really too bad.
He treats me, I declare, as if I were one of his barrack
companions. No matter, though; I shall pay him out
for it one of these days. I am determined to love Edmond a great deal better than him. But the worst
of it is, he is quite capable of never even noticing *that*.
And then, too, I am not quite sure I could do it, even
if I tried. My two dear brothers, I love them both
with all my heart! There can be no most nor least
in such love. Is not one as dear to me as the other?
And only . . . . yes, perhaps—but, God be thanked!
I have them both . . . . if one of my darlings had
never returned, I think it is the dead that I should
have loved the best."

CHAPTER IV.

EDMOND.

EXTRACT FROM THE JOURNAL OF COUNT EDMOND.

" How few among us ever really grapple and close with the great questions of Human Life!

" Here, already passed beyond the boundary-line of man's maturity, I find myself stumbling at the simplest of these enigmas. Here I halt irresolute, hesitating, timid. And I, the man whose brain is burdened with the too, too heavy weight of thought, I am ready to ask my road of a child."   *   *

CHAPTER V.

Felix, Edmond, and Juliet.

Juliet to Theresa.

"L——, 20th June, 1814.

" THE first emotions are over. We have got to be accustomed to each other again, and have grown into the habit of each other's lives.

" It is better so, for it is calmer. Your letter spoke of feelings somewhat akin to these when you told me about your child and your husband, and of your love for these two, and of the difference in that love. How strange it would be did any one become jealous of his own flesh and blood. Is jealousy possible between father and child—brother and brother? But what am I talking of? I meant to tell you something of our lives; how we are all living together here; how quietly; and how happily the days go by.

" Well, then, after breakfast father usually goes out with Edmond, to look over the mills, the farm, the cattle, and see how the crops are coming on. Or sometimes they both take their horses and ride about the forest, to inspect the timber, and that Edmond may see how well and carefully all his suggestions and plans have been attended to during his absence.

" It is really amusing to see how the dear old gentleman behaves on these occasions. He is as eager and as timid as a schoolboy; doubting if he have done well, and impatient for Edmond's approval. Then, when they both come home, I can always see at a glance, by the way he rubs his hands and chuckles to himself, if all has gone smooth and well. As for Felix, we hardly ever see any thing of him before late in the evening. He has registered a vow never to return home without a stag, or some enormous trophy of the chase; and he generally sets out at daybreak, before the house is out of bed. Father is by no means too well pleased with these extensive devastations of Felix just at this season. The other day Felix kept his vow by not coming home all night. Such a fright as we were in! He reappeared, however, the next morning. And in what sort of equipage do you suppose? Mounted on the top of a wooden *charette*, and sound asleep between a wild boar and a stag—a magnificent ten-horner! We all burst out laughing when he made his triumphal entry in this way up the shrubbery, where we were just then taking our morning walk. It was ludicrous to see the puzzled face of him, and the astonished way he rubbed his eyes, and stretched and shook himself like a great dog, before he seemed to know where he was. But, before mother could scold him for the anxiety he had caused us all, he jumped down from the cart, and into her arms, and contrived to pour into our ears, without stopping to take breath, such a long story of wonderful adventures, that no one could put in a word. What saved him, I think, was that it so happened we really were in want of game, for we are expecting a house full of visitors next week. Well, but you must not fancy, Theresa, from all this, that Felix is rude, or selfish, or that he has no taste for any thing but dogs and horses, and shooting and hunting. If Edmond only says one word to him, 'tis enough. He quietly lays his gun by in the corner, sits down as sober as a judge, and in an instant he is quite a different creature; sociable, gentle, and so sweet-tempered and sunny that it is really impossible to be angry with him for any of his numerous misdeeds. Edmond is every thing for him. There is nothing like it. He looks up to Edmond as to a second father. And indeed he may well do so, for he owes him much. Do you know, Theresa, that during the campaign Edmond, though he never studied for the army, at once took the lead of his brother in all the details of military science and practice? All through the war he was the guide and teacher, as well as helpmate, of Felix; and here he continues to be the same in all things. What a surpassing spirit it is!

"Edmond is the most accomplished and complete man I ever met with. What an intellect, and what a soul! Such extraordinary powers of application, such self-possession and solidity of character! Yet he does not seem happy. And this makes me sad. I think Felix is the only perfectly happy creature. He is happy completely. The other, with all his gifts, all his lavish wealth of nature, has yet need of more. Felix is rich with little or nothing. Edmond hardly ever speaks to me now; and I should almost begin to think him indifferent to me if a thousand little nameless silent kindnesses, and acts of thoughtful care, did not prove to me the contrary. And all that he does for me is done so quietly. Felix does nothing at all

for me.   On the other hand, he is always wanting me
to do something for him.   Yesterday he must needs
set me down all the morning to mending his great
leathern shot-belt, which I did, indeed, so well that I
managed, before I was through with that rough, unwonted work, to run the scissors into my finger, and
hurt myself horribly.   Edmond, before Felix even noticed it, was at my side.   He turned quite pale when
he saw the blood on my hand; and, throwing a glance
of disapprobation on his brother, he left the room to
look for some English sticking-plaster.

"But Felix, when he at last saw what was the matter, jumps up, and crying, "Nonsense! nonsense!"
seizes hold of my finger, thrusts it between his lips,
and sucks out the blood so hard that he makes me
cry.   Then, before I can stop him, he catches up the
scissors (the instruments of my mishap), and cuts a
great piece out of my cambric pocket-handkerchief, as
if it were merely a rag of hospital lint.   Therewith he
bound up the wound tightly, and stopped the bleeding in a minute.   I confess that I felt a pain at the
heart when, a minute afterward, poor dear Edmond
came back with the sticking-plaster, and found that
there was nothing left him to do for me.   Felix, in
his rough way, had done every thing.

"'Tis a trifle, this.   But—well, I hardly know why,
Theresa, and yet I have noticed that on these occasions mother shakes her head and steals a furtive, unquiet look at Edmond, as he sits beside us, so quiet, so
self-involved."   *   *   *   *   *

Like this, there are many other letters from Juliet interspersed among the leaves of Edmond's journal. The dates run on to the middle of August. I do not give them all. The selection which I make is enough to throw sufficient light on the interior of these three hearts, happily yet unconscious of the precipice to which an unseen hand was slowly leading them down.

CHAPTER IV.

STRAWS UPON THE STREAM.

EXTRACTS FROM THE JOURNAL OF COUNT EDMOND R——.

"20th July, 1814.

"THE Idea which man calls GOD only exists within the consciousness of man himself. Though we should take the wings of the morning and fly to the uttermost parts of the earth, yet we can find nothing there which we have not carried with us. Whether we scale the heights or sound the depths, mount up into Heaven or go down into Hell, we are equally unable to travel out of our own thought, or attain to any point of space beyond the reach of it. Nay, Space itself and Time are not things, nor even the qualities of things. They are only our manner of thinking of things; the modes and conditions of our consciousness. We are not the masterpieces of a Supreme Being who has formed us in his own image, but our idea of such a Being we have formed in the image of ourselves. We do not resemble him; he resembles us.

*   *   *   *   *   *   *   *   *

The action of all natural forces is spontaneous, self-impelled, independent, and obedient only to the laws of creation. Attraction and repulsion, centripetal and centrifugal force: these are the determining poles of movement. They are the same under every denomination. The conditions of union and disunion are re-

moved from our control within the centres of the inevitable forces that join and part. No extraneous
power prohibits such and such a union. No extraneous power necessitates such and such another.
These two principles are their own employers. The
cause of their activity is in themselves. They create
and destroy at their will and pleasure. In the nature
of man the action of them is spiritual, as in the nature
of the inorganic world it is material. This is the only
difference I can discover.   *   *   *   *

"Hence this lacerating conflict in our own bosoms.
We are the battle-fields, only, if forces we do not
command. Armies whose leaders are to us unknown;
powers we can neither summon nor dismiss, are
camped upon the brain and tented in the veins of
men. The war is theirs, not ours. We are the spectators of ourselves, not the lords. We are conscious
where the conflict is waged. It shakes us at the most
solitary outposts of thought, we are convulsed by it in
the most central abysses of sensation, but nothing of
it is our own save the ravage and the pang.

And man fancies that he is something great because
something great is taking place within him.

So the sun-dial measured out the course of the world
from hour to hour, and it imagined itself to be Time,
and it dreamed that it was destined to become the
compeer of Eternity. But a little cloud was blown
across the sun, and the dial awoke from its dream of
Time and Eternity, and relapsed into—Nothingness.

"As little as the dial could command the sun, can
man command the mind in nature, of which he is the
index; if he dares to think himself more—the dupe.

I

To no force within ourselves or others have we power
to say, 'Be thou thus, and not otherwise; pass thou
here, and not elsewhere.' In no one soul can the fiery
effort of its intensest forces avail to strike from the
soul of another the spark that lights, and warms, and
kindles—*love*. * * * * * * *
* * * * * * *

"Machine or chaos? Behold the conditions of
our being. Is the choice between them always ours?"
* * *

JULIET TO THERESA.

"21st July, 1814.

* * * "Because in my letters I speak so
much of them, you think it necessary to warn me, my
Theresa? Dear, you misjudge. Both of them together are not dangerous to my repose. Either of
them, without the other, might be so. Poised between
these two hearts, the balance of my own is undisturbed. I am at peace because I am in my place.
My life is the necessary complement of theirs. We
three are one. Two of us, without the other, would
be but the moiety of a maimed individuality. Quite
alone, I think no one of us three could exist. Felix
and I are creatures to whom happiness is an instinct
of nature rather than a consequence of conduct. We
act more from tendency than intention. Edmond is
both our measure and our goal. Toward him we
move, and by him our movement is controlled.

"He perhaps, and he only of us three, could exist
alone; for his is the self-sufficing spirit, and his char-

acter is the completest and most finished that I have ever contemplated. Justice, Judgment, Sagacity, Nobility, Power to restrain and refrain, Harmony, Order, Duty—all these are but so many parts of his consummate character. And how difficult to poor Felix is the exercise of these two last qualities!

When the path of his inclination is foreclosed by a prohibition imposed by a duty, nine times out of ten he is sure to behave like a hero; but, alas! when the woful tenth time comes, some rash impulse will often run joyously off with his judgment, and all his previous pains come to nothing. Then he is in such honest despair; he looks so whimsically woful; he puts on such a pleading face for pardon, sits so meekly in his sackcloth and ashes, and is so humble and so sad, that it is not in human nature to be angry with him." *   *   *   *   *   *   *   *
*   *   *   *   *   *   *   *

EXTRACT FROM THE JOURNAL OF COUNT EDMOND R——.

*   *   * "Of all mysteries, it is the most mysterious; of all enigmas, the least explicable. Before the vehement lawlessness of this, all forethought fails; all judgment is disjointed; all calculation recoils or is crushed. In the presence of it, all other presences wax pale and impalpable; by the power of it, all other powers are paralyzed. Yet it is itself impalpable to possession, and powerless to possess. Gratitude, Friendship, Desire—all these we may trace to their sources, and set in motion by our will; but the levers of Love, impenetrable, intangible, are placed beyond

the sight of the eye that is strained, and the touch of
the hand that is stretched to discover them.   And
yet to be master of these is all that can make life
worth having.   *   *   *   *   *   · *   *
*   * So be it then, at last!   Here, where to reason is to be unreasonable, where sense is nonsense,
and all is fatality or frenzy, what farther can I fear?
or why should I scruple to ally Passion to Superstition, weakness to weakness?

"On this lost ring will I stake all that my life has
left to win or lose.   If I find it—and find it I *must*—
then hear me for once and forever, you sightless ministers to man! and be this ring the first link in the
indissoluble chain wherewith to bind her—ay, though
it be forged on the anvils of Hell!   I can no more,
nor otherwise."   *   *   *   *   *   *
*   *   *   *   *   *   *

CHAPTER VII.

DRIFTING.

JULIET TO THERESA.

Extracts.

"FARE thee hence, and fare thee well, thou Unknown Bridegroom!   *   *   Superstition, my Theresa, comes in aid of thine admonitions. My fate is fixed. A maid I remain, for I have lost my marriage ring.   *   *   *   *

"We were playing at ball there. And, the better to hold my racket, I drew the ring from my finger, and put it into my handkerchief, which I had left on the pedestal of the great sphinx that Edmond has had placed in the bowling-alley. Afterward we made up a boating party on the water, and walked home by moonlight through the woods. I thought no more about my ring. But later in the evening, when we were all together in the drawing-room, I noticed that the ring was not on my finger, and immediately ran up stairs to my bedroom to fetch the handkerchief in which I remembered having tied it up. I found the handkerchief where I had left it on the toilet-table, and shook it out very carefully. A little night-moth fluttered, frightened, out of the folds of it, and burnt his pretty velvet wings in the flame of my candle, into which he foolishly flung himself. I think it may have been one of those little sphinx-moths of which,

as you know, there are in summer-time so many, and
such pretty ones, about here.   But I am not the less
convinced that the moth was my betrothed.   The
magic ring must have secretly changed itself into that
delicate, rash lover; for it was no longer in my handkerchief, and has not since been found.

"I have made up this fairy tale to fit my own fancy
as you see, and choose rather to believe myself the
widow of a butterfly than to accept any of the more
prosaic conjectures of all the others here, who still insist in hunting for the lost ring in every nook and
corner tripped over, my Theresa, by the footstep of
thy thoughtless friend.   Thoughtless? yes.   I have
been so.   And now I reproach myself severely, not
for having lost the ring, but for having joked too lightly and too loudly about the loss of it.

"The fact is, I was vexed to see all the world
sprawling about on the ground to look for my missing treasure.   So I cried out, 'Oh pray don't make
such a fuss about it. 'Tis quite useless.   Don't you
know that the ring is an enchanted one, and that it is
destined to chain me indissolubly to him from whose
hand I shall one day receive it?   Now it has spirited
itself away, and 'tis no use looking for it; it will only
reveal itself to him whom I myself am fated to belong
to for time and eternity.   All this is written in the
stars.'

"And these silly words were as indelicate as they
were thoughtless, Theresa; for I noticed at once that
Edmond looked hurt and pained to think I could so
lightly console myself for the loss of a gift which he
had given me with words, no doubt, inspired by a se-

rious and brotherly concern for all that might affect
my future.   Thanks be to my good stars, however, the
fatal ring has vanished.   I persist in believing that
the fairies have changed it into my little winged
bridegroom; and that ill-fated one has been his own
executioner, and roasted himself alive in the candle
of his now disconsolate bride."

*   *   *   *   *

EXTRACT FROM THE JOURNAL OF COUNT EDMOND R——.

"Lost! irretrievably, irrevocably lost!   *   *
*   *   *   *

"And all has been in vain!   *   *   *   *
Man, impuissant in the plenitude of his powers, can
not, then, with the utmost faculties of his soul—with
keenest effort of his will—succeed in commanding the
smallest of those blind and miserable chances that
aimlessly sport with his destiny?   We are mocked!
We are mocked!   *   *   *

"In that cold moment of time when the rising sun
first touched with his pale beam me and the labor of
my long, dark hours, I sickened at the sight and the
smell of the fresh black earth upturned at my feet, and
I shuddered at the imagination of my own image; for
I seemed to be the spectre of myself hovering over the
grave of my hope.

*   *   *   "Yes! I am henceforth the living
grave of a hope that is dead forever.   Gods! gods!
gods! do you look on at all this?   And must we,
too, live on thus, knowing that you know it and are
not sad?   And not any where, any where, any help

—neither in Heaven nor in Hell! We are mocked!
* * *

"Yesterday, to-day, this morning, an hour ago—an age ago—Hope lived. But when he—and *he* ever, and still ever *he!*—he that had not moved a hand, nor stirred a foot—oh heaven and earth! . . . . when the ring which it had robbed from mine, his Evil Genius and my own dropped into his loose, idle hand, then the deathblow flashed in my eyes and fell. * * * Dead! Hope is dead.

"No more praying. What have we prayed for? Let the angels go back to their Heaven empty-handed as they leave us to our earth. * * *

"Night every where, and forever.

"Night on my eyes, night in my soul. And in *this* darkness there is no light but the lurid sparkle of that hateful amethyst. * * It comes and goes, and passes and returns, like a marsh fire on the waste. * * * And They follow it— troops of them in the wicked glare. And I see the grinning of the demon faces on the dark, and I feel the groping and the clutching of the demon hands about the hollows of my heart. * * * * My heart? Is this a heart, this chaos? * * * Felix! Felix! thou—and why thou?—of all others on this mad and miserable earth? Thou *only?* and still ever *Thou!*"

* * * * *

CHAPTER VIII.

AND SOME ARE DRIFTED TOGETHER, AND SOME ARE DRIFTED ASUNDER.

JULIET TO THERESA.

"MY BEST THERESA!—How shall I tell thee, my friend, my sister—what words, even if I could stop to find them, might avail to tell thee all that has happened—all that IS? How surpassing must be my happiness! for if the feeling of it were less rare, there must have been a language and a name for it, and I can find none.

"Yet my hand trembles not; my heart does not beat faster than before. This joy is calm, because it is complete. There is a light upon my soul, and a stillness in my thoughts; and I know, by the stillness and the light within, that the Spirit of Joy is sleeping safe. What birth-throes must bring to the pure and perfect crystal the slowly-formed and darkly-working splendors of the diamond. And what painful agitations, in these last few days even, have preceded the perfect concentration of my heart's complete content!

"Yes, I believe in the magic power of the ring. For surely now—but thou thyself shalt judge, my Theresa, if this old amulet of the Pagan East have not shed benignant influence on one who is now, and henceforth, the very happiest and most joyful child of all the Christian West. Let me tell thee all.

I 2

"Early in the morning of the day after that in which I lost my ring—and my last letter must have then been already on its way to you—we were awaked by the blowing of horns and the baying of hounds in the great court of the quadrangle.   Our neighbors, who were resolved to run a stag that morning, had taken us quite by surprise.   However, mother was up at once, and we both dressed ourselves in haste to receive them.   Felix and Edmond had been beforehand with us.   When we got down stairs, we found the whole party already at breakfast in the armor-room, where a fire had been lighted for them; for the morning was chilly, and the sun only just up.

"Felix was entirely absorbed in arranging the details of the chase.   His picker was standing near him; and it was only at the last moment, when he turned round to take the horn and the hunting-knife from the picker, that he noticed me standing before the hearth, and put out his hand to bid me good-morning.

"The hunting party were just going to start, and one of our guests, as he crossed the room, suddenly exclaimed, 'Why, look at this!   The picture has taken life.'   And at the same time he pointed, laughing, to the old hunting-picture that hangs over the great fire-place—you remember it?—in the armory.

"Every body looked up.   And, indeed, we were all struck by the similarity.   For the picture, as you know, represents, in the life-size, a sportsman, and a lady from whose hand he is receiving, with all the gallantry of attitude which belonged to our grand-father's grandfathers, his belt and bugle-horn.   Really Felix looked the counterpart of the painted sportsman (minus, I need not say, the praiseworthy gallantry of that exemplary image which for half a century at least had been waiting on bended knee for the lady's favor); and I, with a slight change of dress I think, might have very well passed for the Châtelaine herself.

"'Come,' cried another, 'complete the picture, Felix. Down on one knee with you, and let the lady arm you.'

"'Oh!' said I—for on the pavement just at my feet, and between me and Felix, the draught through the open door had strewn a long train of ashes from the hearth—'if Felix kneels to me, he will have to get up again with one knee white and the other black; and he is much too vain for that.'

"'Of course I am,' says Felix. 'But I think one may be gallant without being dirty.' And, taking out his handkerchief, and throwing it on the floor at my feet, with his usual vivacity he flung himself down, with one knee on this impromptu cushion.

"But in the same instant, as though something had suddenly hurt him, his face twitched; and, staggering up, in the effort to help himself on to his feet, he caught hold of a little table that was standing near him, and both he and the table, with all the bottles, glasses, and dishes on it, were tumbled, clattering, on to the stone floor. Felix cut his hand badly with the broken glass.

"Edmond lifted him up, examined the wounds, extracted the splinters, and bandaged up the wounded hand with his handkerchief. But it was swollen and painful; and, finding his right hand quite disabled,

Felix, to his great discontent, was obliged at last to yield to our united remonstrances, stay at home, and let Edmond take his place in the field. *   *   *   *

"They were all gone. The house was quiet. More weakened by loss of blood, and the pain of it, than he would admit, Felix had fallen into a feverish, uneasy sleep, with his head still leaning on my shoulder. I could not move without waking him. So I sat still. Mother was making up some bandages for his hand. We talked on under our breath. She was asking me why the grass and mould had been freshly turned up this morning all round the pedestal of the great sphinx in the bowling-green. I knew nothing about it, but supposed it must have something to do with the loss of my ring, which I had left there.

"'It was perhaps the midnight work of my betrothed,' I said, laughingly.

"At this Felix woke up.

"'Betrothed! Who is betrothed?' he asked, with the sharp, querulous tone of a feverish person.

"'Nobody,' said I.

"Mother left the room just then to look for an unguent.

"I told him all that stupid story over again, with as much nonsense as I could contrive to put into it: How Edmond had given me the ring; the destination of it; and how that destination must remain unattained.

"Felix continued looking at me all the while in a strange, unsettling way, with great, wide eyes.

"'Betrothed!'" he went on murmuring to himself; 'betrothed! And is it possible for you, then, to betroth yourself one of these days, Juliet! And to whom—to whom?'

"I tried to laugh at him, but I could not. He kept looking at me so strangely, as if he then saw me for the first time in his life.

"'And if you were betrothed,' he said, after a pause, 'why then—then you would cease to be my sister, Juliet?'

"'Always, always thy sister, my dear good Felix!'

"I put my hand in his as I said it. But he did not take my hand. He shook his head mournfully.

"'No!' he muttered, 'all would be over then.'

"And so he relapsed into his revery.

"He looked so serious, it made me, too, feel serious. I felt sad, too. I begged him never to talk of this again, for it pained me.

"All at once he started up, and stared at me again with a curious, puzzled look.

"'How was it, then?' he cried. 'Ah! I remember! I remember! Didn't you say yesterday, Juliet, that you would marry the man who should find this magical ring of yours?'

"'Well, yes, I did say that.'

"There my voice broke down. I could not go on. I meant to have added that what I had said I said without meaning any thing by it.

"He became quiet and thoughtful. There was something almost sombre in his face.

"The silence was extremely painful to me. To change the current of our thoughts, I asked him the cause of his fall, and how he came to stumble when he was already on his knee.

"'Ha! yes; by the way—' he said, as if awakening out of a dream.   And he began to rub his knee.

"'Something here,' he said; 'there must have been a stone or a nail on the floor.   I felt it run into me, and I feel the smart of it still.'

"'Your wounded hand,' I said (glad to have found a new subject of talk), 'has made us forget the occasion of it.   Come with me, and let us look together for the cause of your fall.   When we have found the fatal object, whatever it be, we will fling it to the bottom of the deepest well in the house.'

"I took his left hand in mine as I said this, and he let me lead him thus into the armory.

"There we found every thing just as we had left it. The servants, busy elsewhere, had not yet put the room in order.   The cinders on the floor—the handkerchief on the same place before the hearth.   And while he stooped to pick it up, I was looking about among the broken glass to see if any thing had rolled there from the place where he was kneeling when he fell.

"'No!' cried Felix, feeling with his finger and thumb the folds of the handkerchief.   'It is here, in the handkerchief.   I feel something hard here.'

"When he opened it he drew out . . . . the ring! I was speechless.

"We looked at each other in silence.   God only knows what was passing in that moment between our two hearts."   *   *   *   *   *   *   *
*   *   *   *   *   *   *

The next page of this letter is missing.   Perhaps it had been lost, perhaps it had been torn out.   I can't say. I add the remainder of the letter. It begins with a broken sentence, thus:

* * * * "Arm in arm, up and down, as if it had always been so. Then, at last we began to ask ourselves how the ring could have got into the handkerchief. We had returned to the end of the alley, and were standing under the sphinx. Felix remembered, now, that he, too, had placed his handkerchief on the pedestal, and taken it with him when he went away. So I must have mistaken his handkerchief for mine, absorbed as I was in the game. And afterward, taking it for granted that the ring had been lost in the wood or the alley, it never occurred to me to look for it in any handkerchief but my own, where I made sure that I had placed it. The sun was now sinking, and admonished us of the approaching return of the hunters. Father, in his joy, was for announcing our engagement at supper; but mother opposed this idea with a firmness and decision of which I could hardly have conceived her capable. She said it would be most unbecoming to render definitive and irrevocable the step we had taken without first talking it over with him who would one day be the head of the family.

" 'There was something strange,' I remarked to Felix, 'in the tone with which mother said that. And I confess that the thought of Edmond somewhat embarrasses me. For the first time in my life I feel shy of meeting him.'

"As I said this, I fancied I heard a low moaning sound in the underwood; for we were just crossing the skirt of the forest on our way home.

" 'Didst thou not hear it too?' I said to Felix, very

much frightened. And he, too, fancied that he heard
something moving in the bushes. But, after he had
searched the thicket through and through, and could
find nothing, he began to laugh at me for my folly,
and swore that nobody would be better pleased with
the news than Edmond. He talked on with such
hearty, joyous conviction about this, that at last I began to share his confident view of the matter.

"After our return to the chateau, we separated for
a short while to prepare for the reception of our
guests. I had hardly finished dressing before the hunt
came back. The whole house was in a bustle; servants running from room to room-along the corridors;
doors opening and shutting. I got down to the drawing-room as quickly as I could. Felix and father
came in at different doors, very much agitated. Edmond had not returned with the others. The servants were questioned, and had seen nothing of him.
At last some of the hunting party came down, and
told us that Edmond, just after the death of the stag,
had ridden away from the field at a hand-gallop, saying that he had business to attend to in the neighbor-
hood, and they would find him at the chateau when
they came back. Then father remembered that Edmond, when he set out, had said something about taking that occasion to inspect the land survey, who have
begun their triangulation on the other side of the
wood, and are to send in their plans to-morrow. Edmond is so thoughtful about every thing. This re-
assured us, and we went to supper with good hearts.
While our sportsmen were clinking their glasses, however, and devouring their venison like ogres, I could

not help observing how anxiously mother was glanc-
ing every moment at the door and window. She said
nothing; but it was quite dark in the fields outside;
and I saw that she was uneasy, and felt more uneasy
myself than I cared to say. Father's valet came in
suddenly, and whispered something in his ear. I saw
the old gentleman turn pale and start in his chair.
We all saw it, and there was a painful silence. Mother insisted on knowing what was the matter. Father's
only answer was to send for Edmond's groom, who
came in, frightened and confused, and said that his
master's horse had just come back to the stable rider-
less, his bridle broken, and his flanks covered with
foam. .I was just in time to catch mother in my arms.
She tottered toward me, and swooned away.

"All the men made haste to saddle their horses,
and rode away as fast as they could to look after Edmond.

"Felix went without his hat.

"In a few moments the whole house was silent and
empty. Not a sound to be heard but mother's moaning from time to time, and father's unquiet step, pacing monotonously up and down the long, empty sup-
per-room. Each horseman had taken a torch with
him, for the night was unusually dark. There was
no moon.

"I stood helpless, terrified, in the embrasure of the
great window, drearily leaning against the pane, and
pressing my hot forehead flat on the cold glass, which
only made fiercer the throbbing in each feverish vein.
It was a strange, wild scene outside—vast shadows of
the horsemen, as they passed, wavering up and down

on the white wall of the quadrangle, in the glare of
their own torches; the clatter of the horses' hoofs,
and the confused cries of their riders growing rapidly
distant. For a long time I could see the fitful flash-
ings of the torches along the forest. They crossed
and recrossed each other here and there among the
trees like wandering stars. At last they dwindled,
scattered themselves at rarer intervals, and finally
vanished into the darkness. Oh Theresa, what a
dreadful night was that!

"One by one they kept coming back, each with no
good news to tell. The morning dawned at last. It
was heart-breaking. They looked so hopeless, those
livid faces, in the cold, melancholy light. Edmond
had not been to the land survey. This was all they
had been able to ascertain. Some accident must have
happened to him before he could get there.

"Not sleep, but a dreadful drowsiness kept coming
on me at giddy intervals. It brought no rest, but
bad dreams. I thought I saw lying in the long gray
grass, under a hollow oak-tree, the bloody corpse of
Edmond. His brow was crushed and bruised into the
sodden soil. Then I heard again the same low moaning sound I had heard before in the underwood. It
awoke me. I started up. It was the moaning of
mother, who still sat in the chair where I had placed
her, clasping her knees, and rocking her body backward and forward.

"To add to our anxiety, Felix had not yet returned.
A new search was organized. Just as the seekers
were starting, father took my hand without speaking,
and led me into the park. It was still early morning.

We reached the little hill at the bottom of the park
without having exchanged a word with each other.
One can see from the top of it, as far as the horizon,
the whole plain of the surrounding country, traversed
by the winding waters of the Weidnitz. There is a
little wooden bench on the flat of the hill's head.
Father sat down there, and hid his face in his hands.
I drew the dear old head gently against my bosom.
Then, my tears began to fall at last, and his white
hairs were wet with them. Without any settled
thought, I sat thus, with the old man's head upon my
breast, staring stupidly at the cold, cloudy distance
before me. I could think of nothing. My mind had
lost the thread of all things. The tears in my eyes
bewildered my sight.

"On the large white water underneath there was a
small black boat. The boat was lazily drifting down
the sluggish stream. I could not see it distinctly.
The whole land, whitened with the wandering mist,
appeared to be one vast and livid sea. In the midst
of the sea was an open coffin. In the coffin, stretched
at full length, was the corpse of Edmond. The face
of the corpse was sharply set against the hard gray
sky. It was white as marble, but unmarred by any
wound. The features were more placid than ever,
and more stern. All at once the corpse began to
move. It lifted itself, and sat half up in the coffin.
I saw it stretch an imploring hand toward me. I
tried to rush forward to reach it, but could not. Every
time that I endeavored to move, an invisible hand retained me. Suddenly I awoke. The sea and the
coffin had disappeared. I saw the boat drifted by
the current into a bay of the river.

" 'Father,' I cried, 'look! look!'

" I could say no more.

" We both looked, and saw a man rise out of the boat, and step down on the bank of the river.

" It was Edmond.

" How we left the hill I know not. I only remember that we were instantly by the river-side, and clasping him in our arms. Father, for all his joy and all his pain, could find but one expression, and kept murmuring over and over again, as he embraced him, 'Edmond, my boy! my beloved boy!'

" Edmond let us talk on without answering a word. His face was deadly pale. His features were inert; and, being vacant of any expression strong enough to hold them together, they seemed to have no relation to each other. His teeth were chattering, his limbs were shivering, and his eye wandered listlessly over our faces with a heavy, leaden look. It was with the utmost difficulty we could get him to speak of himself.

" Yesterday evening, he said, he left the hunt immediately after the death, anxious to rejoin Felix, whose accident had made him uneasy. He tried to find a short cut to the chateau, and lost his way in the wood. There was still twilight in the fields when he entered the forest; but there the night had fallen already, and the bridle-paths were quite dark. The better to track his way through the thick underwood, he alighted and tied his horse to a tree. While he was still trying to make out his bearings, the horse, restless or frightened, broke loose and galloped off. For some way he followed the noise of the hoofs.

This only led him farther astray. After wandering about in the wood for more than two hours, he heard a noise of waters. He pushed on in that direction, and at last found himself on the banks of the Weidnitz. Then, for the first time, he knew where he was, and perceived that he had taken the wrong direction. He resolved to follow the course of the river, but was hindered at every step by the dense thickets. Worn out with prolonged exertion, he had made up his mind to pass the rest of the night in the wood, when he stumbled over something among the thick reeds along the river-side. It was an empty boat, probably left there by the foresters. With a good deal of difficulty he got it afloat. He found that it would hold out the water.

"There were several pine-trees in that part of the forest. He cut a branch from one of them—the longest and straightest that his hunting-knife was strong enough to cut. With this he tried to punt the boat down the river; but the waters were so swollen that the spar was no use to him. Then he lay down in the boat, and let it float him down the stream without attempting to guide it. The cold on the river numbed him, and he soon lost consciousness. The grating of the keel against the shallow bottom of the little bay, where it touched land, was the first thing that aroused him.

"'Oh, Edmond,' says father, 'if you knew what anxiety you have caused us! I wish you had trusted the instinct of your horse: it would have brought you home safely. Those beasts can find the stable at any distance. And such a night as we have had of it!'

"Edmond answered nothing, but only dropped his head lower, as if he was weary of the weight of it. That man, so strong, so inured to fatigue, seemed broken by the work of a single night.

"'Well,' said I, 'we mustn't scold him. See how ill he looks, father, and how weary!'

"'True, child, true! go in first and prepare mother!' father said. So I went in before them. Oh, how glad I was to be able to tell her!

"You guess, dear Theresa, how great our joy is now! I would not close this letter before I was able to give you this best news. Felix, who had returned before us, was almost beside himself with the joy of it. But my eyelids are beginning to drop, and I am very, *very* tired.

"Thank God, Edmond is safe! How soundly I shall sleep now! Rejoice with us, dear friend. Good-night!"

CHAPTER IX.

THE INTERIOR OF A SOUL.

I SUBJOIN six pages from the Journal of Count Edmond:

FIRST PAGE.

" When I started the beast on his road with a stroke of my riding-whip, I thought—So be it, Death! there goes thy messenger. Let him snort his good news at the doors I shall not enter . . . .

" 'Fear no more. He will not return to frighten you. He will never come back. Fear no more, young lovers. But, if you would never see him again, then, when you two walk arm-in-arm about the pleasant places, heed well that you walk not near the hollow oak; for there, when the grass is black, and the useless blood is filtering through the dead red leaves, his face might vex you if you chanced to see it.'

" What power was it that held back my uplifted arm?

" Was it that puissant impuissance—cowardice?

" How, fool! can that man be a coward who trucks a life of torment against the short, swift stroke that brings the long release?

" Was it filial piety?

" Blaspheme not!

" Not in that moment didst thou think of father nor of mother.

"No!

"It was something more deadly than the flash of the suicide's knife that glimmered up from the dark, false heart of the water.

"It was the violet flame of that accursed amethyst. I saw it kindling, keen, vindictive, in the sullen depths. I saw it fawning, crawling, in the fiery ripples. The spell of it was on me. My eyes were the slaves of it. Looking at it was listening to it, for it muttered and muttered as of old. The light talked to me; and the little waves hissed and lisped,

> "' *Where hast thou the stone ? where hast thou the ring ?*
> *Thou art ripening, brother, and ripening.*'

"And I shuddered not. I was not afraid, for the voices were familiar to me.

"I had heard them before.

"There was a promise in them which I dared not construe.

"But I trusted it.

* * * "What seekest thou here? Why lingerest thou in the way of wholesome human life? Why walkest thou thus among honest men ?

"There is mischief in thee. Thou bearest the sacrilegious thing in thy bosom.

"Fly !

"Fly while there is yet time. Fly to the uttermost distance; away from all men; away from thyself. Thou art marked and signed. Fly !" * * * *

SECOND PAGE.

"Woman !—Eternal schism in the soul of man ! Robber of his strength, which yet strengthens not thee! Thief of his will, which yet confirms not thine! Who gave thee—and to what end, if not to thine own hurt—this power upon us? Thou needest not to exert it. We bring thee (we ourselves) our own defeats, in that conflict wherein he that is overcome is the only one that has fought. * * * *

"Year after year, hour by hour, how have I lain my ear to the most secret cells of thy sweet being, and listened to the budding pulses of its bounteous growth! How all the tender germs of thy soul's beauty have been my heed and charge! And how I thought to tend them, and to train! For every secretest seedling of thy so lovely spirit, I knew what Nature needed, and could antedate the blossom in the bud. How inexhaustible seemed *then* the lavish opulence of beauty yet to be, within those ripening germs, spread out before the forward-looking eye of my far-gazing and shortsighted love!

"And now?

"A summer wind—a breath—perchance a waltz, has fixed thy fate and mine.

"What know we? By the ways we watch, Loss comes not; but it comes.

"And perchance—perchance, in the swimming tremors of a dance, some drop of lighter blood, some pulse of brisker motion, has signed the contract with the Gardener of this Paradise—a Hussar!"

THIRD PAGE.

"Death. Ending. Annihilation.

"This is all I can see at the extremity of every avenue. All paths lead to it, none beyond it. Thou

K

hast suffered that thou mightest suffer—nothing more
—nothing else.

"Of what dost thou complain?

"Thou wouldst live—thou hast lived. Who promised thee more than this?

"I would live? Did I ever ask for life? When
have I ever said (and to whom?), 'Open to me the
doors of Life; I wish to live?'"

"Never, never, at any time have I said that.

"Who has assumed this right over me?

"What can force me to keep, against my will, this
property in pain which has been gratuitously thrust
upon me?"   *   *   *

Fourth Page.

"How deep the roots have struck!

"All that must be torn up, only to find the traces
of it deeper, deeper still!

"To retrack, laboriously along the devious inclination of a life, each of the long, long stealthy by-paths
whereby this yearning Spirit has stolen into our heart,
secretly, silently, unguessed, there weaving into its in-
extricable web fibre after fibre of the soul's imperish-
able stuff!

"And now to cut out the rooted garden of one's
life, patiently, painfully, spade in hand—the labor of
the grave-digger!

"And how *can* I?

"In the sorely sensitive places, where the latest
wounds are fresh and raw, new blood spirts up from
deeper down; the wrenched nerves quiver with in-
extinguishable life; and, deepest down of all—deep

down among the remotest sources of Being—the youngest eyes of Childhood are gazing, weeping up to me; weeping—'What harm have we ever done thee?'

"No, no, not this. I can not do it. Not *this!*

"Weep on, sweet innocent stars, weep on.

"What harm have ye ever done me?

"I know not. But *ye* I can not harm, sweet eyes!

"Rest ye, rest ye, childish angels! rest ye in your silent spheres unvexed. What know ye of the anguish that is moaning round you? What know ye of the wrongs that reach so near? Rest!

"To you, oh quiet eyes—dear friendly stars of the far off early time, that look unconscious kindness still —I will turn my own for refuge from my latest self.

"Far off, far off, in the holiest haunts of Memory, I will build me a bower for Oblivion."

Fifth Page.

"I have never looked on life but as a task; never completed, ever renewing itself, in each accomplishment creating fresh undertaking.

"So be it, then, even this time also.

"However inconceivable, however unendurable may be the life to which my soul is awakened, yet at least *she is awake.*

"Pause not, poor Soul, to contemplate the ruins of thy so wondrous fabric of the former time. It is shattered. Thou canst not reconstruct it. See, these littered shards upon the sordid earth! Here lie they, all thy loving unloved labors—the once aspiring shafts, the airy pillars, the kingly key-stones—ruined, defeatured shapes of Beauty and of Strength, whereon thou didst scheme, and dream, oh Soul, to plant the Dome of thy Felicity. .

"Build not, build not!

"Presume not to be the architect of thine own happiness.

"Pass on.

"Yet say . . . . 'The plan was good and fair. Majestically moulded in the inmost mind, daintily fashioned, and delicately decked by all the richly-ministering Hours; how bold, how beautiful, how bravely built, how firmly settled upon fast foundations, how sumptuously solaced with all noble color and harmonious form; with what brightening toil, at what tender touchings, the temple rose, like mounting music, upward, ever upward to the golden cope, the glorious consummation of the perfect plan!'

"But there Bliss settles not.

"She will not dwell in the house that is built with hands.   Free as the bird of heaven, she soars from the hand of God; she hovers in the happy air; she 'lights upon the trembling bough.   There, poised upon the yielding tremor of the tender stem, amid the dancing leaves, she sings her magic song.   And while thou listenest, upon lightest wing she flies away.

"Build not, build not!

"It comes and goes by other laws, this Happiness, for which we labor and so late take rest.

"Sleep!—deedless, aimless, vacant, unmindful.

"And on thy dreaming head the airy thing will perch unsummoned.   Know it not.   Fear to recognize it.   Whisper not its name.   Soon as thou callest it thine, thou hast lost it."

SIXTH PAGE.

"With fire from what far-off heights, in glory of light how divine, and with what holy heat, there streams into my soul the clear conception of the sublimest image that man can contemplate on earth!

"Divinest DUTY!

"Thou that art to the soul as a trumpet sounding from another world—thou in whose untroubled depth of strenuous calm is reserved for the consciousness of man its only consolation, and for his conscience its sole rest—who dare dispute thy prerogative? What else on earth may presume to be thy peer? Thou only, large and sovran Shape, canst fill the perfect orb of Contemplation; thou only, solitary regent of the loftiest law, art worthy to hold unshared dominion in the soul of man.

"For thou art Certainty.

"Where thou standest, there is the vanishing point in the long perspective of deeds; and, whatever the course of the line, in thee is the law and the end.

"What, oh Soul, thou hast power to behold, that thou hast power to be. Seest thou Certainty? It is thine.

"Never shalt thou bring to an end the superhuman struggle. Never at any time shalt thou be able to say of this or of that, 'Enough, it is finished.'

"Regret not; rejoice not; endure.

"Dare not, oh wrestler, to say, 'I have overthrown.' The foe is ever before thee. The cause is unending, eternal, one with the Godhead. Thee no price can pay, no recompense reward. Be thou the creditor of claims unsummed, whose compt can never be quitted, for the value of deeds wherein dwells a grandeur too proud to be impoverished by profit.

"Renounce. Sacrifice. Suffer!

"For. what?

"For a gain to be gotten? for a price to be paid?

"What? wilt thou barter sorrow for joy, as a huckster goods for gold?

"Sad were the bargain; for thou art rich, but thy life is a pauper.

"Lock up again, poor world, thy proffered pension for pain. How shalt thou appraise me the price of a pang made perfect? What conditions canst thou add to that which is complete? or what recompense aread to the rejection of reward?

"Fain would I know in what coin of comfort thou wilt weigh me the worth of a consciousness made costly forever by eternities of anguish contained in the triumph of a moment.

"No. The farewells of the soul are immortal.

"Now is Forever.

"The felicity rejected from Time has no admittance to Eternity; for Eternity *is*—not *is to be*. Therein is neither past nor future; and these are the conditions of requital.

"Nothing is durable but the duty to endure. Duty is the asylum of the soul.

"Oh Venus Libitina! Oh Beauty, beautifying graves! Oh Keeper of the registers of Death! Thou .sittest among the sepulchres, yet art not sad. And 'Here,' thou sayest, 'there is calm.' I will believe thee. Yet there is a chilly pallor on thy brows, and darkness in the circles of thine eyes. Thou, too, hast struggled. * * *

"And to this cold goddess, that to her, also, gracefulness may not be wanting, the great Founder of the world has lent, for coy companion, Beauty's humanest handmaiden, Chaste Shame.

"Vex her not with words. Silence is the chastity of action.

"Let no cry be heard. Crush the escaping groan on the yet quivering lips of the desires thou hast strangled. Uncover not the pale faces of thy departed. Utter not their names aloud. Know thyself, and bear to be unknown. Strike down this beggar heart that prowls for alms, and stops men's pity in the public place. Justify the whole endeavor in the perfect deed. Slay thyself and hide the knife.

"Even so. And as, in large compassion of fond eyes young graves set grieving, kind Nature makes mute haste to cast over the hillocks of the recent dead her grassy carpet of the tender green, so silently, and for others' sakes with such a noble haste, do thou, too, hide beneath the serenity of a smiling face the sorrow of thine immortal soul!"

CHAPTER X.

Samson Agonistes.

How far the preceding page of the count's journal is a faithful revelation of the actual state of his mind at the time when it was written, may be judged by the following fragment. For the impartiality of the testimony herein contained, the unconscious character of the witness is the best guarantee.

Juliet to Theresa.

"I am thankful to say that our anxiety about Edmond is over. His vigorous constitution has triumphantly resisted the feverish attacks which at first alarmed us. Though no longer suffering, however, he looks more serious and preoccupied than I ever saw him before. But my timidity and reluctance to tell him of our engagement were utterly unjustified, and I could now kneel to him for pardon for that momentary foolish shyness.

"When father, in our presence (after his recovery), made known to him the vows we had exchanged, my heart fluttered so fast, and I felt so frightened, that I dared not meet his eye, though I felt he was looking at me. But Edmond answered at once, 'What, dear friends, and do you think that this is news to me?— to me, who have known ever so long—ay, long before you suspected it yourselves—that you two dear ones belonged to each other?—to me, whose fondest wish is thus accomplished? and who, indeed, have only waited for this long-expected moment to tell you all that I, too, have made my choice, so that there will soon be three families living together, and loving each other, at L——.'

"This news, and, yet more, the joyous manner of it, took us all by surprise. We pressed him to tell us more. And—but this is a profound secret. Have I the right to tell thee? Yet why not? I well know thou wilt rather banish it from thy mind than let it pass thy lips. Well, then. Thou knowest that centenary lawsuit about the Rosenberg property near Oels? The present possessor is childless. The heiress is his niece. And this circumstance is sadly in the way of the Rosenberg claim. Proposals have been privately made to terminate the dispute by marriage. The object of Edmond's last visit to Breslau—thou thyself, I doubt not, didst not suspect it any more than we—was to see the heiress. He now tells us that the sight of her has confirmed the favorable impression made by all that he had previously heard as to her character and education. And he assures us that his mind is made up. But nothing is settled as yet.

"You know with what caution and deliberation Edmond acts in all things.

"In my secret heart am I glad of this arrangement? Frankly, no. I understand not this sort of marriages. Indeed, this decision of Edmond's would be quite unintelligible to me if my knowledge of his character did not enable me to understand that to him marriage,

K 2

under any circumstances, would be the result of a decision dictated by considerations of prudence, after mature deliberation. Well, be it so. I am not made to understand it. But when I see a young girl like this poor Rosenberg heiress, and when I must think, 'There goes she in the grace and gladness of her youth; and some poor girlish fancy no one cares to suspect can bring a softness to her eyes and a flushing to her cheek, and for any little pleasure—the unconscious kindness of a careless word; some peasant's greeting as he holds back the silly branches in the cherry-orchard not to touch her as she passes—the grateful blood will brighten as if to show how easily young souls are pleased, while her heart beats quicker at the sound of a step she knows'—and then, when I must think that all this while she knows not, poor child, that in point of fact she is nothing more nor less than an Old Lawsuit—well, I say that saddens me, Theresa."

EXTRACT FROM THE JOURNAL OF COUNT EDMOND.

"Impossible!

"I can no more. Nature can only concede to the possession of pain the limits of her own strength.

"Lord God in Heaven, look down upon this soul which Thou hast made. See how it fares with Thy creature.

"What is there in this single solitary sentiment to justify the tormenting tyranny of it, when I confront it with all my proud projects, of which each seemed large enough, and lofty enough, to fill grandly a great life?

"What is it?

"A wish.

"What to me is a wish?

"Miserable mendicant, have I not denied thy claim? Bankrupt bill, drawn with fraudulent pretenses by the need of a moment upon the poverty of an eternity known to be insolvent, I have torn thee! I have canceled my name from the bond. I have done with thee forever.

"Why, then, art thou here again? Why comest thou back to me disguised?

"More fearful art thou in this, thy present form, because less false, than in that other. Lie as thou art, yet hast thou in thee now the terror of a truth.

"For now thou hast forsworn thy plausible pretendings. What art thou now? Less, and yet more. Nothing, every thing. Less than a Wish, yet more insatiable—a Longing. Thou believest not, affirmest not, dost promise not, any more. Thou lookest where there is nothing to be seen; thou walkest where there is nothing to reach. Spurred by the conviction of the unattainable, thou travelest, empty, into emptiness. Seeking for seeking's sake; motion without a meaning; travail without birth; a race without a goal.

"What have I to do with thee, womanish wooer of unmanly souls? Rank, unwholesome weed of weak self-pity, insinuate not into the pulses of my life thy crawling roots.

"Impalpable impostor, thou art detected and denounced. Only as a wish couldst thou dupe the credulity of a mind diseased. To the eye of the hectic the face of approaching Death is florid with the hue of Life. To the sickly sight the sunset seems the sunrise, and decay's red signal blushing health. Only to a mawkish sense, thou feeble Longing, canst thou look like Hope. But I am strong. I know thee, and I will not know thee. Away!

"Or rather, in thy real form, thou Protean monster of the many faces, reveal thyself at last. Take palpable substance, that I may kill thee. Come forth! avow thyself! I know the hellish name of thee at length. Appear! Be seen, for what thou art, in thy most loathsome shape, detestable Lust. Blight, even in the body of the brute! Procurer to the tiger and the ape! Shall I cringe to a thing so vile? Shall I stoop to a force so foul?

"Beastly, abortive fiend! Fasten thy mad-dog's bite into my living flesh: not a groan shalt thou wring from the scorn of my soul in her wrath. Unshamed in the consciousness of all that I am, unquelled in the kingdom of myself, undebased in my dignity of man, dare but to stir, and I strangle thee dead!"

CHAPTER XI.

How it strikes a By-stander.

Letter from Joachim Furchtegott Schumann (Agent and Property-Intendant of Arthur Count R——, of L——), to Baroness Theresa N——.

"L——, 15th September.

"Honored Madam,—As in duty bound, with profound respect, I take in hand my humble pen, in order to acquaint your honor of the sad calamity with which it has pleased God to visit the noble family of my honored lord and esteemed master, the count. Also, honored madam, it is by the express orders of his honor that I make bold to pen these sad lines, for his honor is in hopes that your ladyship's esteemed presence may alleviate the bereaved soul of her honor the Lady Juliet. May it please your honor to pardon your honor's dutiful servant if, in the recital of this sad tale, as in duty bound, I occasion great grief to your ladyship's kind heart.

"Yesterday, 14th *hujus; scilicet* the day of the Elevation of the Blessed Host, being about the hour of 8 A.M., and the morning cloudy, it pleased the two young lords, my esteemed masters, to go duck-shooting down the river. And it was their lordships' intention to cross same river, *videlicet* the Weidnitz, from the point of the long bend beyond the old mill, which is at the distance of about three quarters of a mile,

under correction I say it, as near as can be, opposite
to the great marish, which also is well known to your
ladyship.

"The keeper's lad was with their lordships in the
boat (which is a likely lad and an honest, as your
laydyship knows), and they let the dog run after them
along the bank (which is a black retriever bitch).

"May it please your ladyship, the young Lord Felix, my honored master, was uncommon gay upon the
morning of this melancholy occasion, being high in
his spirits and exceeding cheerful, as was remarked
by said keeper's lad. The same deposes that while
his honor Count Edmond was at the rudder, his hon-
or Count Felix, being at the bows, and having got his
feet astride upon each side of the boat, continued,
there standing upright, with great mirth and joy, to
rock the boat upon the water. But his honor's brother, my esteemed master, Count Edmond, seeing this,
with great seriousness besought his honor to sit still
in the boat, and not to do this thing, for that the water is uncommon deep in that part, and that, if his
honor should fall over, he might not be able to swim
by reason of his heavy shooting-boots. Nevertheless,
the young lord, for the great cheerfulness that was in
him that morning, made light of all that his honored
brother was saying to him; for he only laughed very
pleasantly all the while, declaring that these heavy
water-boots seemed to him as light as a pair of danc-
ing-pumps.

"Now at this moment it happened, honored madam,
as I am duly informed, that a hind rose in the brakes
by the river-side, and the dog (which is a young dog,

and a bit wild, but will do better when broke, as shall
be duly done) ran out after the hind, and would not
come back to call. So then the young lords, having
landed the lad that was with them in the boat (as
aforementioned), bade him fetch in the dog, and meet
their lordships about a hundred yards lower down the
water, just opposite the marish (as above). The lad
tells me that while he was running after the dog he
could hear for some time the laughter of my honored
and lamented master the young count. It was a quarter of an hour before the boy could bring in the bitch,
which, when done, was well punished, as duly de-
served. The same then repaired to the place as above
indicated; who, when there arrived, with great surprise beheld the boat already far down the stream, beyond said point, drifting, and quite empty. But of
the two young lords was no trace apparent, near nor
far. At first the lad thought that their lordships must
have landed and gone up the marish, and that the
boat, being ill fastened, had got adrift. So he waited
some time, and fired off his gun; but neither to this
signal, nor to all his shouts and cries, was there any
answer. Then, looking all about him in great perplexity, he at last noticed that there was something
hanging on the branch of a willow-tree this side of
the great fen. And when the lad went up to the willow to see what this might be, then he recognized the
hat of his honor Count Felix. At that sight the bitch
began to howl. Honored madam, among all the folk
in our parts, specially sportsmen, this is much thought
of for a grievous bad sign, which it was no better,
honored madam, on the present melancholy occasion.

Then the lad felt uncommon low in his mind; and, crying and weeping bitterly, he ran back to the castle, where he caused great alarm. May it please your ladyship, the writer of these humble lines, your ladyship's dutiful servant, happened to be upon the spot, and, taking with him a few followers, hastened to the fatal scene. There, having got a punt afloat, we tried with long poles to search the bottom; but the stream was running stiff, and I lament to say our search proved fruitless. By this time the banks on each side were filled with folk. Also, honored madam, many went up to their necks into the water; for no man thought of his own life for the great love that is borne to the noble family of my lord the count. At last, then, some of the folk which was about in the water began to shout and call to us that were in the boat, who, coming to the fatal spot, nigh about ten paces from the bank, all black and befouled with mud and slime, as was grievous to look at, being also dripping wet, my honored master Count Edmond. The same was quite insensible. His face was buried in the black ooze, and his honor's hands convulsively clasped behind his head, as if he had there flung himself in great despair, which was a sight full piteous to behold. But of his honor the evermore-to-be-deeply-lamented and now happily-at-rest Count Felix, up to this day, honored madam, no trace whatever has been found.

"His honor's bereaved brother, my deeply afflicted and highly esteemed master, Count Edmond, is uncommon distressed and troubled in his mind, so that the exact details of the above-mentioned melancholy occurrence can not yet be ascertained. For his honor, as is well known to your ladyship's kind heart, was most uncommon fond of the young lord his brother, so that, for the great sorrow and heaviness of his heart, his honor is still, under your ladyship's pardon, as I may say, almost beside himself. It appears, however, only too certain that the young lord must have fallen into the water while he was rocking the boat; and his lordship's brother must have tried desperate hard to save him, for his honor's clothes were wringing wet, and his boots were so shrunk with the water that we were obliged to cut them off his honor's legs. Furthermore, honored madam, the count's clothes were full covered with weeds and gravel, through which his lordship must have dragged himself while searching for the defunct at the bottom of the river.

"In terminating these sad lines (and may it please your ladyship, without his honor's express orders I should not have made so bold to put pen to paper), I have also the honor to inform your ladyship that I have ordered relays of horses all along the post-road, in order that your honor may reach the castle as speedily as possible. With the most profound respect, as in duty bound, so far as the melancholy circumstances will permit, I am, honored madam, your ladyship's humble and dutiful servant,

"JOACHIM FURCHTEGOTT SCHUMANN,

" *Gräflich R——scher güter Inspector.*"

BOOK III.

The Fruit of the Seed.

In the same hour came forth fingers of a man's hand * * *.
Then the king's countenance was changed, and his thoughts troubled
him.—DANIEL.

BOOK III.

CHAPTER I.

After the Event.

THUS far I have been able to let the count's papers speak for themselves. A great portion of the succeeding pages, however, is occupied with irrelevant details; and I have therefore thought it convenient to reduce the substance of these pages into narrative form, extracting only such passages as appear peculiarly significant.

If any one well acquainted, in other and happier days, with the chateau of Count R—— and its inmates, had revisited that household after the date of the letter transcribed in the previous chapter of this book, he would have been struck by the fragility of those foundations upon which human happiness is built.

The grief of the count and countess for the death of their youngest son must have acutely increased their anxiety at the precarious state of their eldest and only surviving child.

Insensible to the presence of all around him, Edmond wanders, restless and solitary as a spectre. Whole days he passes alone in ever the same spot

upon the river bank, watching with glassy eyes the
rolling waters. At nightfall he glides home, shadow-
like, among the shadows.

In the old drawing-room, once so cheerful—there
where Juliet's joyous song and Felix's merry laugh
are missing now—wan faces in the heavy twilight
hours peer at the melancholy windows, or through
the doors no greeting enters. When night is falling,
the woful watchers at those windows see a lonely
figure here and there about the ghostly park restless-
ly wandering. When night has fallen, and the silence
is heavy on the house, the poor pale listeners at those
noiseless doors can hear a dull and leaden footstep on
the stairs. It passes the door which no hand opens.
Edmond goes straight to his own chamber, and shuts
himself in. All night along the floor of that chamber, monotonously backward and forward, the same
dull, leaden footstep sounds. They can hear him muttering to himself in those short incessant walks, and
sometimes groaning loud.

Suddenly a great change comes over him. Still
taciturn and more than ever self-involved, but calm
and quiet as before, he resumes the daily regularity
of his previous occupations. At earliest dawn his
horse is at the door. The whole day long he is busi-
ily engaged about the property. Accompanied by
the inspector, he visits every part of it; sets all things
in perfect order; and makes such careful provision
for the future as would seem to imply the purpose
of a prolonged absence.

In the course of a single week, as I find, he was
three times at Breslau. The next week he goes there

again. This time he does not return. Three days after his departure, the coachman who drove him there comes back with a letter which he is charged to deliver to the old count. In this letter Edmond takes leave of his family in terms which indicate, chiefly by the exaggerated effort to conceal it, a violent grief, violently repressed.

With vehement bitterness of reproach, and in words often incoherent, he accuses himself of the death of his brother. Life has become to him an intolerable burden. He can not hope for relief of mind so long as he is surrounded by scenes which remind him every hour of that terrible accident. He announces his departure for St. Petersburg. It is his intention to enroll himself in the Russian army, now on active service in the Caucasus. If he should not return, he implores his father, and mother, and Juliet to let their forgiveness rest upon his memory, etc., etc.

None of the family is much surprised at this decision, nor at the language in which it is announced.

Though Edmond has nothing whatever wherewith to reproach himself, yet it is easy to understand how naturally, how inevitably the mere fact of having been sole witness of a calamity so sudden, and of which the victim was so nearly related and so dear to the survivor, must have planted into every bleeding memory thorns which a conscience so delicate, and a nature so severe in the criticism of itself as those of Edmond, would be impelled rather to drive deeper in than to eradicate. All had felt the absolute necessity of change of scene for Edmond. But that he should have chosen a remedy so sharp would doubtless have grieved them more, had not the excess of a previous grief already blunted those susceptibilities which are most prominent to pain.

In the spiritual no less than in the physical world, the maximum of power resides in the infinitely little.

As the surface of the globe is changed at last by the gradual crumbling of the hills; as continent is severed from continent by the slow small toil of multitudes of softest water-drops washing the sides of the world; as from the bosom of the deep rise up new continents of vast extent, whose coral-building architects might be covered by millions in the hollow of a man's hand, so, also, in the economy of the life within us, the constant and uniform recurrence of little things at last irresistibly establishes the durable basis of Habit and Custom. In this consists the healing power of work. And in work itself, as well as in each man's faculty to work (second only to religion, and the faculty to apprehend and employ the presence of a Divine Comforter), is the highest blessing bequeathed to man by the helplessness of his nature. For man is a day-laborer, paid by the day and the hour; not for the thing done, but for the doing it. He can not command results; he can not comprehend the plan of the Architect; he can not always choose either his place among his fellow-laborers or the materials given him to work with, but he can always do a day's work, and earn a day's wages.

So it was with these three poor mourners in the old house at L——. Hardly two years had passed away. A superficial observer might have seen nothing to remark about the inmates of the chateau beyond the fact that the habitude of a tranquil sadness had settled itself into the vacant place of a peaceful felicity. The chateau had become a convent. But in the one as in the other, life followed its natural and necessary course, reflecting now more of the inside, as it had formerly reflected more of the outside world. The only tangent at which the sphere of this closed and inner world came into contact with that of external circumstance was in the one point of Edmond's distant lot.

At first, for some time after his arrival on that theatre of war, once the cradle of our race, his letters had been few and brief. As time went on, they became more frequent and more full.

Remarks about the manners and customs of those primordial tribes; descriptions of the nature and scenery of that country; observations upon the analogy and relationship of languages—that fine but firmly-woven thread which traverses, throughout millenniums of change, the confused history of man, and unites, by almost imperceptible fibres, the end with the origin of human culture—such are the contents of this part of the journal and letters of Count Edmond, which indicate only by the different names of the places from which they are dated the participation of the writer of them in the events of the war. He himself never speaks of these events. That he was concerned in them, and that he survived them, is proved by his letters; that this was almost a miracle is proved by the details of the official bulletins of the Russian army in the public journals of that time.

At last came the spring of 1817, and with it the first warming ray of hope and comfort to the hearts of those who read these letters by their cheerless hearth at L——.

Edmond has announced his return in a long letter to his father.

But amid the pulses which this announcement quickened in the old man's heart was one to which a message from a yet more distant land had already said, "Thou shalt be the last."

One day, when this letter of Edmond's had been joyously discussed at the dinner-table at L——, the old count died in his chair while still at table. He died of apoplexy without pain, and his eyes closed on the hope of his son's return.

So that it was now as lord and master of L—— that Count Edmond returned to the house of his fathers, and there were *still* three mourners in the old chateau.

But the firm, deliberate footstep which now sounded on the stair, and over the long silent hall at L——, was no longer that of a boy. Whatever of masculine power had hitherto slumbered unemployed in the dreamy character of the young count, two years of martial strife and toil, the hardy life of a barbaric camp, and long resistance to inclement weathers, had now ripened into complete development. His tall, spare stature; his sinewy frame, suppled and hardened by constant bodily exercise and endurance; the smooth metallic lucidity of his firm and finely-chiseled features, embrowned and fortified by long exposure to wind and sun; and that severe suavity and gentle sternness of manner which is only the attribute of men who have fought down violent passions, and conquered the prerogative of a strict reliance on their own powers—all these, in their accumulated impression, gave to the bearing of Count Edmond that accurate smoothness and strong consistency of power which the sculptor demands from the bronze to which he confides his conception of a demigod. The large regard of his luminous and quiet eye, naturally soft and plaintive, had also acquired an intensity and depth, which lent to the spiritual expression of his whole countenance a placidity that might well pass for the repose of a soul at peace with its own passions. In all the manner and appearance of him at that time there was, according to the unanimous testimony of eyewitnesses, that lordly, unobtrusive, but irresistible self-assertion, which is the characteristic of those who, from the habit of controlling themselves, instinctively control others, and assume unconscious but undisputed precedence in the great Ceremony of Life.

His influence upon those around him was the greater inasmuch as, during the last two years of absence, he had either acquired that rare tact, or developed that yet rarer natural quality, which graces the submission of one will to another, by giving to it the appearance rather of a spontaneous homage than of a conscious concession.

There are some natures that are like suns. Place them wherever you will, they instantly become the centre, and control the movement of all things. This inborn faculty of control exists quite independently of age, or experience, or social position, or intellectual power. You often see a child of six years old ruling by right divine an entire household; and nothing is

more common in public life than to find men of no
surpassing capacities, whose names never appear in
the newspapers, but who nevertheless exercise paramount and permanent influence over the master-minds
of their time.

The most striking novelty in the present conduct
of Count Edmond was that he now spoke with perfect frankness and marked frequency about all that
was still most painful in the events of the past.   So
far from avoiding allusion to these recollections (upon
which, in the minds of Juliet and his mother, two
years of silence had settled undisturbed), he seemed
rather to seek for every occasion to dwell upon them.
And, in doing this, he contrived with such singular
skill to make these yet sore subjects the accustomed
ground for constant interchange of ideas, that day by
day, and little by little, they at last began to arrange
themselves, under his guiding and constructive touch,
into the consistent parts of a picture, the general effect
of which, if pensive, was at least not painful, as daily
more and more at the touch of a master-hand the new
and brighter lights that grew out upon the foreground
softened the harsh outlines, and melted them imperceptibly back into the long perspective of the past.

If by such means, on those occasions which he had
acquired the faculty to create, Edmond, with unwea-
ried assiduity incessantly, either sketching in new objects, or dexterously completing with consummate art
such faint unfinished indications as he chanced to find
already on the canvas, contrived by slow degrees to
engage the interest of Juliet, by, as it were, drawing
her into counsel upon every detail of that work of

which she was herself the unconscious subject; if he thus accustomed her mind to tend more and more toward external action by giving to her feelings, hitherto buried in the seclusion of her own heart, the long-missed charm of participation, and the indefinite comfort of an interest which he had the art to make appear the spontaneous result of her own volition; if, I say, in the daily continuance of these delicate and kindly efforts, Count Edmond relaxed nothing of that patience which commands and justifies success, who can be very much surprised that within a little more than a year after the count's return to L——, when at last the old countess rejoined her husband, when Edmond and Juliet stood together by the grave of their common mother, and the death which thus reunited the old seemed to bequeath to the young couple a life insupportably solitary if not henceforth united, Juliet could find in her heart no voice to oppose the voice of Edmond when it pleaded for that union—not with the passion of a lover, but with the pathos of an old and faithful friend?

And this plea was urged with such perfect abnegation of all personal desire, such quiet resignation of whatever happiness was beyond his power to claim or hers to grant, while every reason for compliance with it, to which the exclusive consideration of her interests might have prompted Juliet, was so delicately employed by Edmond in favor of his own, that she was innocently drawn to regard as a noble duty and a sacred sacrifice the step which in no other sense it would have ever occurred to her to take. Instead of saying, "*You* are an orphan," he said, "*I* am an orphan." Instead of speaking of the relations between them as a solace to which she had accustomed her daily life, he alluded to them only as a source of saving strength which he himself was too helpless to resign.

Thus it seemed as though the curves in which these two lives were moving, having at first run almost parallel, and then diverged far asunder, were bound by natural laws to rejoin each other in completing the perfect circle.

CHAPTER II.

MATED OR CHECKMATED?

BUT in the innermost soul of Edmond all was not so peaceful as the smoothness on the surface seemed to indicate. It appears from many of Juliet's letters that the habitual placidity of his self-composure was sometimes inexplicably disturbed.

In one of her letters, written about this time, I found the following passage:

"The fatigues of his last campaign, however, must have shaken Edmond's health to an extent which, in despite of his extraordinary powers of self-restraint and endurance, he can not quite conceal. There are moments when his face suddenly becomes white and bloodless; his eye settles in glassy fixity upon a single spot; the wonted composure of his features is disturbed by a fearful spasm; he stands as if horror-struck, his lips convulsively compressed, his chest violently heaving. These attacks are, as he himself assures us, the results, happily now rare and rarer, of a violent fever, occasioned by a dangerous wound, which nearly proved fatal to him in the Caucasus. He fancies, and not, I dare say, without reason, that the coarse remedies and strong drugs of the Russian military physicians have proved even more detrimental to his constitution than the fever itself. These fits, he says, are very painful, but not at all dangerous. I shall never forget one evening when, for the first time, I witnessed this strong man, so habitually master of himself, completely convulsed by one of these strange seizures.

"The night was wild and gusty. An autumn storm was howling outside. There were long sighing noises about the house. One could hear the doors creak wearily in the empty upper rooms, while the dead leaves, blowing up the windy avenues, and whirling round the house, kept up a continual patter on the window-panes, like the tapping of elfin fingers. Edmond and I were playing at chess. Mother was dozing in her arm-chair by the fire. I need hardly tell you that Edmond is much stronger than I at this game. But he has the talent to equalize our forces by calculating to a nicety the value of the pieces he gives me, so that I can almost fancy myself at times a match for him. That night the game had lasted longer than usual. I really think that we were both in earnest, and each of us doing his best to win. For the first time, I seemed from the very outset to have divined the plan of my adversary's battle, and had so arranged my game that, whenever he tried to catch me, I was ready for him with a counter-move, on which he evidently had not reckoned.

"At one moment he seemed to have quite lost patience. Strange how eager this game can make one! It really tries the temper. Seeing him so excited, I too, on my part, put out all my strength to escape his attack, which was boldly conceived and hotly pressed. He was so resolved to harass my Queen that his usual caution failed him; and, by an oversight, he laid his King open to my game.

"At last, however, he made a master-move with his King's Knight just as I thought myself sure to check-mate him. I was so vexed by this disappointment that I had a strong mind to upset the board, and was just on the point of doing so, when suddenly, as if by enchantment, the whole game appeared completely changed. A single piece had achieved this miracle. A Castle which I am almost sure I had been keeping in reserve, well protected in a corner of the board on my enemy's side, was now standing out in full check to Edmond's King. I did not notice this piece in its new place till Edmond had withdrawn his hand from the board. I thought at first that it must have been accidentally displaced by his sleeve; but this could hardly have been the fact, for there were other pieces in the way which, in that case, he must have upset. I certainly felt sure that I had not moved the piece my-self, and how it got half across the board without my noticing it is to this hour a puzzle to me. I had not time to make it out; for all at once I was struck by the appalling change in Edmond. His face was dead-ly white, his lips blue, his eye wild and haggard, and his whole frame convulsed and shivering.

"To add to the strange horror of this fearful meta-morphose, mother, who was dreaming in her sleep, suddenly began to mutter,

"'Yes, yes, Felix, I know—I know!'

"I tried to assist Edmond, who had risen from his chair, but he waved me away with his hand, and stag-gered out of the room, feeling his way with both hands along the wall like a blind man.

"I never told mother about this attack of Edmond's,

L 2

but I asked her afterward what she had been dreaming about, and repeated to her the words she had uttered in her sleep. She had forgotten every thing, however, and did not even know that she had been dreaming. We have never played at chess since that evening. This game frightens me."

CHAPTER III.

JULIET'S RELIGION.

AGAIN, in another letter, which, though undated, I have no difficulty in referring to the same period, Juliet writes,

"I begin to think that Edmond is trying to hide from us the real cause of these attacks, and this makes me anxious. I fear that the frightful recollections of the 14th of September must at least have something to do with them, and that all his heroic efforts and long self-exile have not yet sufficed to dissipate every trace of that cruel shock. I can perfectly understand this. For the first time in his life Edmond has found himself, as it were, confronted with Providence, and compelled to recognize the operation of a will higher than man's, independent of man's, and inscrutable to human understanding. Ah! dear Theresa, we may ignore the love of God, we can not ignore the power of God; and how dreadful would be the power without the love! I have no doubt that, in the impotence of his efforts to save my lost darling, Edmond must have felt the omnipotence of the great Disposer; but it is in his nature to regard himself as responsible for the failure of those efforts. For Edmond is not a religious man. I know that. At least he is not religious in our sense, nor according to our way of feeling. His character is noble and lofty in all things, but child-

like and submissive in none. His intellectual pride
is unbending. I do not presume to judge him on
that account. Men's minds are differently constituted
from ours. With us women, the heart acts upon the
mind, and we think what we feel. With men it seems
to me that the mind acts upon the heart, and they feel
what they think. Thus we get to conclusions quicker than men do, because with us conviction is the result of feeling, not of thought; and feeling is instantaneous, whereas thought is progressive. But I do not
believe that either the woman who feels rightly, or
the man who thinks rightly, will act wrongly.

In old days I used often to talk with our dear father about this religious indifference of Edmond.

Father had a way of explaining and justifying it,
which made a great impression on my mind, because
he was himself a man of unblemished piety and un-
shaken faith. Certainly Edmond from his earliest
years evinced an extraordinary independence of judgment. He would never adopt a second-hand opinion
without having first severely examined it. In this
his mind is singularly conscientious; and I have oft-
en heard father say that, even as a boy, Edmond used
to astonish him by the weight and precision of his remarks. He will have nothing to do with enigmas.
Whatever coincides not with the perfect structure of
thought, whatever is not amenable to the strict law of
the understanding, he does not absolutely reject, but
he refuses it admission to his mind, as being beyond
the province of the intellect. According to him, the
mind of man can only operate within certain limits,
and whatever exists beyond these limits does not ex-

ist for the mind, because the mind can not take cognizance of that which it has no means of verifying. Edmond is no scoffer, however. He denies nothing. For he says that the possibility of denial involves the possibility of affirmation; that the mind is not competent to deny what it is incompetent to affirm, and that we are only entitled to affirm what we are able to prove. He fully admits that there exists in man an indefinite desire, a vague longing, which impels him toward the unknown, and renders him susceptible to the mysteries of religion. He also finds it quite natural that this want, like every other want, should have a tendency to satisfy itself; nay, even that the want of any thing indicates the existence of the thing wanted. But if the satisfaction of this want is only possible *by* faith; and *in* faith, and not possible by any process of thought, or in any logical demonstration of fact, then (he would say) it presupposes in man a faculty which he may possess (though how or whence he knows not), but which he can not acquire. After all, this is not very different from what the curé says himself when he talks of Grace and Election. Only I can not help hoping that grace must come by prayer; and if I rightly understand what Edmond means, I suppose he would say that prayer *is* grace—a faculty not to be acquired; and this is a chilling thought.

"I remember father used to say that unfortunately our sublime religion has not been always carried out in conformity with the Divine origin of it. And, surely, he would say, a dogma which is based entirely on love should never appear beyond the reach of love. In following out such a dogma, a child might be our guide. And was not the Savior of the world himself

a child? And, in all worldly matters, did He not remain a child, even to the Cross? 'Ah! children,' father would say, 'name me the man that ever offered
himself up to be crucified for the love of all mankind.
Alexander the Great? He died of a fit of intemper-
ance. Julius Cæsar? He fell an unwilling victim to
his own ambition. Yet these men have been exalted
to the rank of demigods, and held up to us as great
examples. Or the Philosophers? Pythagoras, to
whom Divine honors were paid? He lived chiefly
for himself, and shunned the vulgar. Or Zeno, dying
in hale old age, to whom was voted a brazen statue
and a golden crown? Or Epicurus, whose birthday
was honored with annual festival? Or Empedocles,
who flung himself into Etna for vanity's sake, and to
cheat the admiration of the world? Or Plato, who
took care of his health and died painless? . Or Soc-
rates, best and wisest of all, who was sacrificed by the
Athenians? Even of *him*, can it be said that for deep
love of all the human family he sought and died a
torturing death?

"'No, no! the power of Christianity is in the sacrifice of Christ. The whole Christian precept is in the
Christian deed. But this has not been adequately
borne in mind. Doctrine has been added to doctrine,
while example has dwindled out of sight; and, while
all history teaches the power of religion upon the
spirit of man, every page of history proves how that
power has been perverted to worldly uses. While
the Church has been building up her establishment,
Faith has been left to shift for herself. Yet the
Church has more than once been shaken to her
foundations, while Faith has never lost her hold upon

man. Well, then, how can we wonder if the children of these later times are born, and grow up, and live in doubt? They are the inheritors of a vast superstructure, the growth of successive ages, which is bewildering even to contemplate, which is a maze of incongruous architectures, and which they must nevertheless take as they find it, without diminution or addition. But, while this edifice has been growing in all directions, the sacred fountain of which, after all, it is only the shrine, has been neglected and over-heaped with ruin. Yet we are bidden to maintain every stone of the temple for the sake of the old well-head which the temple is choking and hiding.'

"In this way father would gently extenuate Edmond's indifference to religious dogma, and, rather than blame him for lacking conviction, he praised him for honestly endeavoring to substitute, for convictions which he could not conscientiously profess, a strict and exact adherence to the duties imposed upon him by the noble severity of his own judgment. 'And so,' he used to add, laughing, 'we may let Edmond alone for the present. For the future I have no fear. The day will come when love, the grand teacher of us all, will enter my boy's heart. Then the scales will drop from his eyes. Let him but once realize that true and fervent love which asks nothing for itself, which is chiefly blessed and beautified in the bounteous consciousness of the existence, the holy contemplation of the worth of what it loves—that love which makes men's thoughts religious and men's hearts child-like—then you may be sure that his hands will involuntarily clasp themselves in a prayer that will need no prompting from without.'"

CHAPTER IV.

SIGNS UPON THE ROAD.

ONE other extract from these letters of Juliet, and I hasten to drop the curtain on a picture which would not have been so long obtruded on the reader's attention but for the significance of its relation to the events immediately to be recorded. The following extract contains the account of a circumstance, to which, in connection with others of the same nature, Edmond himself alludes in that paper which came by chance into my hands on the occasion of my accident in the Bois de Boulogne. The letter from which it is taken must have been written about a month before the death of the old countess.

"Edmond, who had long been free from all attacks, lately alarmed us exceedingly. This time mother was with us, and saw what took place; but fortunately she only saw in it an accident. I saw more, and was dreadfully frightened; but this event has really proved our salvation, and I now recognize in it the hand of Providence, which uses evil for beneficent purposes.

"It was a fine warm afternoon. Edmond had engaged us to drive over in the pony carriage to the old water-mill by the Giant's Seat. He himself accompanied us on horseback, sometimes riding by the side

of the carriage, sometimes on before. He had promised us a pleasant surprise. I must tell you that Edmond, with great skill and taste, has succeeded in
bringing all the most beautiful views about L——
within the circle of the park itself. The old straight
carriage-drives have been done away with, or so
changed that they now wind in and out among the
busks and thickets, sometimes plunging under deep
masses of foliage, sometimes sloping into long green
vistas, or breaking upon lovely open views.

"After winding about in this way for about three
quarters of a mile through the great copse at the bottom of the Home Park, we came quite unexpectedly
upon a view of the mill which was entirely new to me.
Unawares, and silently, the thick foliage had fallen
away from us on either side, and we found ourselves
upon a high grassy terrace overhanging the ravine.
The scene was as enchanting as it was unexpected.
To the right uprose black, abrupt, and bare of herb-
age, like the side wall of a world, the Giant's Seat. A
vast white cloud was settled in slumbrous masses on
the summits. It was the mellowest hour of the afternoon, and the whole bosom of the snowy vapor was
bathed in golden light. Higher up, the warm sky
was in its deepest blue, and the height of the rock's
steep flank had the strange effect of seeming to give
unusual height to the heaven itself. Above the rock,
and above the cloud, in that deep blue dome of breeze-
less air, two brown hawks were hovering and wheel-
ing. Over the long and thickly-foliaged gorge a broad
veil of transparent purple shadow was drawn slant-
wise from base to summit, slicing one half of the op-

posite slopes from the languid yellow light that still leaned downward from the edges of rich green. Hutched among the gray and dewy slabs, in the bloomy bottom of the glen, the old brown mill was crouching by his spectral wheel. Swift from the cloven summit high above, down sprang the shining water-serpent on his prey. There was no sound in the warm hollow but of the shattering of the long cool water, and the groaning of the black-ribbed wheel, which, caught in that foaming coil, kept spinning from his dripping web tissues of dropping pearl and diamond sparks. But underneath, the violent water-spirit, appeased by previous exercise of power, lay at large and at ease in a placid pool of vivid emerald, about whose basalt brinks burned brilliant clusters of the bright red moss. Half way up the glooming mountain-wall a phantom prism came and went, and rose and fell, at fitful intervals, as ever and anon the floated smoke of throbbing spray was tossed into the sun a hand's-breadth higher than the extreme slope of the sunless air beneath. The spirit of the stillness was melancholy, not morose.

" We could hardly bring ourselves to relinquish the luxury of admiration with which we lingered in this charming spot. But the afternoon had deepened round us unperceived, and at last Edmond, reminding us that we had still to visit the mill itself, pushed on his horse toward the mountain road which he has lately constructed, and made a sign to the coachman to follow. I leaned back in the carriage, pensive and dreamy. There was a soothing softness in the early autumn air. At that moment the heavy burden of memory seemed lightened, and the ever-present past more tolerant of peace. Something in the view we had just been admiring had drawn my thoughts toward Edmond; for, indeed, this view has been almost called into existence by his artistic skill. He was riding on before us slowly. He never looks more to advantage than on horseback. At the junction of the old carriage-drive with the new road, which runs along the flank of the Giant's Seat, there is a finger-post, which now came into sight at the bend of the valley, with its long arm and stretched forefinger pointed at us, almost as if it were trying to warn us back. So, at least, I have since fancied. Edmond was just in front of the finger-post, and going to turn the corner. Suddenly he gave a faint cry. I saw the reins drop from his hands; I saw him fling up his arms and put his hands before his eyes. He reeled back in his saddle as if he had been shot, and the next moment he was stretched upon the ground senseless. We jumped out of the pony carriage and ran to assist him. The groom, too, who was following, rode up in haste and alighted.

"While we were still stooping over Edmond, we were all terrified by a tremendous noise close to us. We looked up. The mill had become invisible. Hardly a hundred yards before us an enormous fragment of rock, covered in a cloud of white dust, lay sheer across the road and barred the passage. The ponies took fright, turned round, and dashed homeward at full speed. Fortunately, the carriage upset, and this enabled the coachman, who showed great presence of mind, to stop them and bring them back.

All this while we were about Edmond. He soon came to himself, and none but I had any suspicion of the true cause of his fall. I, however, who had seen one of these seizures already, could have no doubt as to the nature of this one. For the rest, thank God! he was not in the least hurt. Before the groom could come back with another carriage, we had time to examine the landslip. The wall to the right, along the new road, is only just built. The workmen had not given it sufficient support. It had broken down, and a vast fragment of rock, which had been displaced to make room for the road, had fallen with it, just at the moment when, but for Edmond's accident, we should all have been passing under it, and must in that case have been infallibly crushed to death."

CHAPTER V.

EDMOND'S RELIGION.

I NEED add nothing to these extracts. Here, then, is the point to which this unhappy man was come. No matter how strongly he might strive against it, he remained a prey to the mysterious action of a Power unknown to those around him, and incredible to himself.

In vain (his journal proves it) did he endeavor by every means in his power to convince himself of the impossibility of apparitions.

THE HAND was there.

The spectral amethyst still smote him with its violet rays.

Not always. Not when he wished it. Not by expressly exciting his imagination could he bring it before him. For this he had often tried. Since, if he succeeded in this (he thought), then the spell would be broken; then he might analyze the nature of the vision, investigate the causes and conditions of it, and rest sure that whatever he was able to evoke by power of will, he should always be able to dismiss by the same power.

Not being able to do this, he hoped to accustom himself to this spectral visitant which he could neither summon nor exclude; and he labored to render the thought of it familiar to his mind. Labor lost!

When the last apparition already seemed to him as a half-forgotten dream; when, in the full enjoyment of untroubled health, and the clear consciousness of intellectual power, he might reasonably assume that he had fairly rid himself of a temporary nervous irritability, then, by ways the most unexpected, and ever with increased significance, IT returned.

In the mid-heart of the barbarous battle, in the treacherous solitude of the mountain ambush, had he not seen that hand put aside the gun that was leveled at his head? Among the balmy autumn woods at L——, when not the shadow of a cloud in heaven gave omen of the sure destruction to which a hundred paces farther must have brought him, had he not recognized the lurid ring upon the stretched forefinger of that posted arm, imperatively warning him back? And once before, over the chessboard, when he had boasted to his own heart that Juliet could not escape him, had it not crossed his game, and found a means to let him understand that it, the Spectre, would know how to balk him?

Would the thing execute its menace? Would his be always the only eye to see the apparition? Or would it, at some later time, reveal itself also to others? These were the doubts that assailed him. So must he live on.

He had built up for himself an elaborate edifice of internal law, suggested by, and based upon, the analogy of the visible organism of forces acting on external nature. In this system the relations of cause and effect were so close as to admit no place for passivity. Action only was considered capable of consequence.

Causation could not exist in that which had no action. The thing that was not *done* was not at all. What effect could be attributed to that which itself had no existence ?

In this circle of ideas his mind continually moved. I find proof of it in all he wrote.

This is why the inscription on the Egyptian ring had so strongly seized upon his imagination. His own thesis had arisen from the tomb, fortified by the authority of twenty centuries. This is why he had so cautiously considered each active expression of his will, so scrupulously weighed every action of his life. As, according to this way of thinking, the sum of effects must be equal to the sum of causes, and as he thought that he could precisely predicate the first if he carefully calculated the last, he assumed for certain that he could never become the slave of a passion; since, passion being only an *effect*, had he not beforehand measured and assigned to it its definite extent by the exactly equivalent limits accorded to the *cause* of it in his proper action ?

In the same way he reduced his responsibility to a similar equation. So much action, so much responsibility. He would suffer himself to recognize and accept no responsibility which was not contained in (and legitimized by) this equation. To his own law he had strictly adhered. The law of his mind he had made the law of his nature. He had never evaded it, never opposed it, never flinched from it. In this he had sought security, and to this he now clung with the energy of despair. In his own sense he had never failed, never been wanting. He had, under no provocation, ever humiliated himself in his own eyes. He dared not do so; he could not do so; for, in this system of his, he had left himself not so much as a foot's breadth for escape from failure. A system which did not admit of weakness could not provide for pardon. By the side of his law was chaos: one step beyond his inch of solid ground, the abyss. Mediation was impossible where there was nothing intermediate. At the summit of his severe religion, in the place of a compassionate Christ, stood a relentless Necessity.

CHAPTER VI.

Before the Altar.

It was the day fixed for the marriage. It had been settled that the ceremony should take place in the private chapel of the chateau, and in the presence of only a few witnesses—the most intimate friends of the family.

Edmond had long looked forward to this moment. He felt that it would be the decisive crisis of his life, and he was forewarned that the Spectre would appear. He was resolved to confront it without flinching. By resolutely fixing in his mind the thought of the apparition, he sought to prepare himself to sustain, undefeated, the shock of that sudden terror, of which the triumph is—madness. It was neither of Heaven nor of Hell, but of himself, that he sought strength for the final conflict.

When he felt that he was master of himself, he went to meet his betrothed.

Those that saw him pass said to each other, "See how brave and hearty is our young lord to-day! How gallantly goes he yonder, with his manly step and handsome face. On him Heaven's blessing visibly reposes; for he is of a noble nature, and 'tis written clear on the brow of him that there is not in his veins one drop of sullied blood."

M

But none of them could see the stormy brewage that was working deep under that serene exterior.

Those who have ever visited the silver mines at Freiberg or the Hartz will be familiar with a fugitive and beautiful phenomenon which occurs during the process of melting the ore, and lasts but an instant.

The miners call it *silberblick.*

When the air first comes into contact with the incandescent liquid mass, there is seen for a moment a bright iridescence of vivid colors in rapid motion. This brilliant phantom is produced by the impure alloy, which, under a light whitish cloud, suddenly combines with a particle of the oxygen in the atmosphere.

The metallic mass, seized with a twirling movement, manifests variations more and more rapid, and shines with the shifting light of the most beautiful evanescent tints. Suddenly all movement stops. For an instant the molten metallic surface loses all its lustre—looks dull, opaque, and dead. Then there is a farther change; and instantaneously the same surface is completely overspread with the smooth clear polish of the pure silver. Under the influence of intensest heat, all the particles of foreign matter have been dissipated. But at the bottom of the melting-pot they have left a trace of their passage—a small black spot.

The miners say, "*Reine silber blickt nie.*" (The *pure* silver has no *silberblick.*)

The fire, finding nothing more to consume, leaves —on the surface, a smile; in the interior, a raging heat; deep at bottom of all, a black spot.

This is the *silberblick*.

When Edmond stood before the altar at the side of his betrothed, there was a smile upon his face.

It was the *silberblick*.

For his thoughts were not in the sanctuary. He saw neither the priest before him, nor the bride beside him, nor the witnesses around him.

He was waiting for the Spectre. He was arming himself for a supernatural combat.

He knew It would appear; and, for the first time, his own spirit felt itself a match for his ghostly assailant. Nothing—not even the movement of a muscle —betrayed that this man was challenging with superhuman defiance the whole world of spirits to banish that smile from his face.

All his senses were sentinels, vigilantly on the watch. He was throwing out scouts and outposts in every direction. He was making his great reconnoitre. He peered into every corner. He heard the slightest noise almost before it was audible. Before him, around him, here, there, every where—ay, even outside among the corridors, and in the porch, the park—there where eye and ear withdrew their aid, his nerves, stimulated to the highest pitch, had forced into his service a new unintermediate sense, wherewith to meet midway, and so forestall, the onset of his phantom foe. Should he succeed in this—should he, by a supreme effort, contrive to forelay the apparition before it appeared, then victory was assured to him. The Ghost would have been beaten before it could come into the field.

And all this while he was standing there—the altar

before him, his bride beside him, all eyes upon him—standing there, smiling, erect, placid, with his wonted noble air of easy power and unstudied grace, free from all apparent effort, free from all apparent fear, and yet withal as beseemed that sacred place and solemn hour, in reverent attitude before the minister of God.

Now is come the moment of the benediction. Now the priest invokes the bride and bridegroom to join hands.

Now, surely, It must come?

Calling up all his powers, setting all his battle in exactest order, once more Count Edmond scrutinized with keenest insight every nook and cantle of the chapel. Wherever a shadow could lurk, wherever a single ray of dubious light could steal, behind every column, along every wall, probing each crevice, sounding each chink, following each mote in the sunbeam, searching each shade on the flintstone, he sent forth his spies and informers.

Nothing.

Now he could dare it. Now the Spectre was baffled—banished. The stealthy thing had not been able to find unguarded a single cranny in the material world whereby to enter in, and storm the citadel of the soul.

He put forth his hand to join the hand of Juliet in eternal union, and—

It was *there*.

There. In the hand of Juliet, the hand of his brother Felix.

Courage! Flinch not, man! Flinch not now! It has come. It is here. The Ghost has kept his word.

He tried to pluck those dead man's fingers out of the hand of his betrothed.

He could not.

The amethyst kept him off.   The amethyst shot at him its spiteful burning beams.   The amethyst hissed at him with its scorching whisper,

"*Disturb not the Hand of Destiny.*"

His will rebelled, and audaciously issued its commands.   Every limb of his body was paralyzed, and refused to obey.

The priest pronounced the sacred words, and blessed the union of the pair.

What pair?

Edmond heard and saw all.   Mechanically his lips proclaimed the inviolable vow.

For another.

For a dead man!

CHAPTER VII.

EDMOND AFTER THE MARRIAGE.

THE ceremony was over. The nuptials were concluded.

Edmond had kept the promise he had made to himself. He had not flinched. Not a muscle had quivered, not a nerve had revolted from the dominion of that iron will.

But he felt that he was now at the end of his tether. His strength was exhausted. His blood, so long and so severely restrained, now beat and surged with savage power against the walls of his brain. His brain boiled.

He still saw clearly before him, but what he saw was fearful to be seen. He knew where he was—on the brink of the abyss. He knew whither he was going—to the deepest depth of it.

He was perfectly conscious that he could, at the utmost, only purchase a few more moments of self-control at the price of insanity.

These moments he could accurately calculate. He counted them up, and knew the exact sum that he could still dispose of.

With a hideous clearness of intellect, with an atrocious self-suppression, he conducted his young bride to the great banquet-hall, where the assembled guests were now waiting to felicitate the bride and bridegroom.

With unruffled composure he received their congratulations. He had a gracious look and a well-placed word for each and for all. Urbane and placid, he withdrew himself from the hall.

Making a sign to his valet to follow him, Count Edmond, with a firm footstep, regained his own apartments. They were at the extreme end of the house.

With his accustomed tranquillity, and in a voice no tone of which was shaken, he then said to the valet,

"I give you four minutes. Go, fetch me here four lackeys, or four of the stable-men—the tallest and strongest you can lay your hands on. Let them bring with them rope and cord—the stoutest that can be found, and plenty of it. Make haste."

The valet was accustomed to obey orders promptly, and without answering. Like master, like man. Count Edmond's serving-man was too well trained to permit himself on any occasion the impertinence of surprise. He was the most decorous of valets to the most decorous of counts. He bowed and withdrew. At the end of four minutes he was back with the men and the cords. Had his master told him to fetch four hangmen and four halters, he would have done his best to give satisfaction.

The count bade his servant turn the key in the door.

He did so.

Edmond was standing at the foot of his bedstead. His right hand was closely wound about one of the ponderous pillars of twisted oak which sustained the ceiling of the bed. It was an antique bed, richly carved and heavily curtained.

The face of Edmond was livid.

"Bind me—quick—the hands—the feet—quick!"

These words came broken, one by one, in a dry, unnatural voice, from his lips. He was breathing with
difficulty.

The servants stared at him, stupefied, speechless.
He did not speak again with his lips. His lips were
locked, and his nostrils inflated. But his eyes spoke
fiercely—entreaty growing into menace.

Still the servants hesitated.

Then the bed began to creak and crack.

Suddenly the great bedpost, wrenched from its
socket, flew up, spun round, and dashed against a
large plate-glass mirror, which it shivered into splinters. The ceiling of the bed crashed in, and fell with
a loud noise.

The dike was broken.

And the hideous overflow, no longer restrained or
impeded, surged and seethed into every limb swollen
with the strength of a giant.

It was only after long and furious struggle that
those four athletes were able to subdue the madman.
At last they bound his limbs with cords, and laid him
on his bed, panting, exhausted, senseless.

Before leaving the chamber, the count's valet, who
had not lost his presence of mind for a moment, imposed upon his four astonished subordinates the most
solemn pledges of secrecy as to all that had happened.
The count's apartments occupied the farthest portion of the least frequented wing of the quadrangle.
Across the locked double doors no sound could have
escaped to the other parts of the house. The valet

guessed that his unfortunate master, in his last moment of lucidity, must have counted upon this. When
he had exacted secrecy from the four grooms, he left
them in charge of the count, and quitted the room.

He was gone to look for the countess.

M 2

CHAPTER VIII.

JULIET AFTER THE MARRIAGE.

JULIET, also, had retired early from the guest-chamber.

Her mind was absorbed by a gentle melancholy; and, taking with her Theresa by the hand, she sought for relief to her feelings in conversation with her friend.

So the two women sat together, and talked on, in low tones, to each other; Juliet leaning on Theresa's bosom, and clasping Theresa's hand, and the quiet sunlight on the serious faces of them both.

"Indeed, indeed, dear friend," Juliet said to Theresa, "I have well weighed the weight of this day, and the worth of it. I have long been asking myself whether what is now done was right and fit for me to do, and I have convinced myself that my duty lies here. Do I not owe it to Felix to remain by him that remains, faithful to him that was ever faithful and true; him that Felix loved so inexpressibly — him whose life has been so strangely saddened by the loss of that beloved brother? This is what was in my mind this morning. I wished to set myself clear with my own heart; and when Edmond met me with such a holy calm upon his noble features, I blessed God that I was able to devote to him all my remaining life. But tell me, my Theresa, tell me, you who know all

my heart and all my life, whether in this I ought to
reproach myself: when I stood just now before the
altar, I felt separated from all around me, and my
thoughts were of Felix. Again I seemed to hear
those unforgotten words which he said to me in that
first moment when our eyes were suddenly opened
upon each other's hearts. Again I seemed to feel his
arm about me, and to hear his voice, '*Never now, Juliet, can I leave thee. Here or there, in time and eternity,
I am thine, and thou art mine.*'* When the priest
blessed our union my feelings were strangely sad,
strangely happy. The hand of Edmond, when he
placed it in my own, was as cold as a dead man's
hand; but at the touch of it I felt my whole frame
thrilled by a sweet sensation which I had not felt for
years. I had felt it first, and felt it only, long ago,
when I used to walk with Felix hand in hand. I
was overpowered by these recollections. I dropped
my eyes toward the cold hand that was clasped in
mine, and, oh Theresa! I fancied in that moment that
I saw there my lost bridal ring—the ring I gave to
Felix, the ring which Edmond had given to me; but
the strange, unintelligible characters of it moved out
of the visionary stone which I seemed to be seeing,
and twined themselves about in sparkling violet light,
like little fairy snakes, and wandered over both our
hands like luminous veins; and the veins branched
onward and upward over my whole being, and my
life-blood seemed to be flowing through them, and
they lighted up the interior of my soul. Multitudes

---

* These words were probably recorded in the missing page of Juliet's letter, p. 207.

of fairy rings in bright succession, and by the last
links of all in the sparkling spirit-chain our two hearts
seemed united; for in that moment's dreaming I
dreamed that it was Felix still beside me—still the
hand of Felix that held mine. Then, when thrilled
with a faint, strange joy, I looked up in my husband's
face, I noticed with what deep devotional intensity of
gaze Edmond was clasping my hand, and I understood, then, that Edmond was become one with Felix
by his union with me, and that thus the schism of my
heart was healed, and all was reconciled and hal-
lowed."

Juliet's friend smiled at these dreamy fancies. And
she too said "All is well, and all is reconciled."

Nor was there need, she said, of any fairy snakes
from phantom rings, since now, in a new and earnest-
ly accepted duty, the true links had been found, which
also should, by faithful exercise of pure and wholesome feelings, be made fast.

So Theresa thought. And Juliet, she said, should
not any more be brooding on this buried past, but
must now exhort and encourage her own true heart
to seize and sanctify the sober verities of this daily
human life, wherein it behooves that we should stand
firm upon our feet, that we may not be overcome by
the gust of accident.

At that moment the valet of Count Edmond entered the room.

CHAPTER IX.

The Field of Battle.

THE valet had not been able so completely to efface from his clothes and his countenance all traces of the recent struggle but what the two women were alarmed by his appearance the moment he entered.

They both rose before he could speak, and cried in a breath, "For heaven's sake! what has happened?"

"He is quite calm, and he sleeps," the valet said.

And, prudently suppressing all details of the scene he had just witnessed, he hurriedly explained that his master had been seized by a violent attack of nervous fever. He had already sent for the nearest physician; and he conjured the countess not to go near her husband till she was authorized to do so by the doctor, since, in the first stage of nervous fever, any emotion might prove fatal to the patient.

Juliet was with difficulty persuaded to obey this injunction. But she yielded at last to the earnest entreaties of Theresa.

It was well for her that she did so.

For behind the doors she was was forbidden to enter, Horror was in full possession of his own.

Here was the scene of the count's last battle and irretrievable defeat. The strife had been stupendous; the defeat was overwhelming. Inch by inch, with inflexible patient audacity, the man who there lay corpse-like, crushed, utterly beaten on that hideous battle-field, had usurped his own liberties in conquering one by one the antagonisms of his own nature. He had left to the realms of his spirit no law but the despotism of an elaborate tyranny. He had succeeded, for he had reigned. On every part of his being he had imposed his power. His success was his failure. All at once, and all together, the banded forces he had long enslaved revolted and overwhelmed the usurper.

Napoleon had found his Waterloo.

The field of battle was strewn with wreck and ravage. Broken furniture, fractured limbs of costly chairs and tables, bruised morsels of gilded frames, shards of precious porcelain, shattered mirrors, horrible splinters of glass, shreds of ripped and tattered drapery, were heaped in dreary disorder all about the tumbled room, and over the soft carpet, in whose rich pile large earthy footmarks still bore witness to that scuffle of brute strength with brute strength.

In the midst of this miserable litter, his clothes torn, his eyes bright with dry unmeaning fire, his lips smeared with spume and blood, bound hand and foot, upon his broken bed lay the most urbane and knightly noble that ever justified the primæval prerogatives of aristocracy.

And around him, breathless, pale, with blood-spots on their bruised cheeks, with their coarse lips cut and smeared, and their brawny knuckles red and raw, stood his conquerors—four burly, low-browed sons of the stable and the out-house.

Theresa had quickly interpreted the sidelong sup-

plicating glance of the valet. As soon as she could
safely leave Juliet, she found a pretext to quit the
room and rejoin the servant, who was waiting in the
antechamber to conduct her to the count's apartments.
She felt herself responsible for all that was now to be
done, and did not lose her presence of mind.

She ordered the servants to remove the broken furniture, and set the room in decent order. She had
thick curtains placed over the windows. She in-
structed the valet to get the bed put together, and to
cover the sick man, who remained bound and senseless.

While this was being done, she descended to the
guest-chamber, and excused the absence of the count
on the ground that his wife was slightly indisposed.
This, as she had anticipated, induced the wedding
party to break up and withdraw. When the house
was empty, and the last coach-wheels ceased to grate
the gravel at the gates, she returned to Juliet.

"Thy cares come early, my poor Juliet!" she said;
"but sooner or later care must come, and we must do
our best to bear it."

Without giving her time to reply or give way to
alarm, she began to prepare her friend for the per-
formance of the duties which might now be required
of her.

Meanwhile the doctor arrived. He questioned the
witnesses of Edmond's attack, had a long secret conversation with Theresa, examined the patient carefully, and declared that the count's strength was completely exhausted, and that for the moment no new
outbreak of *dementia* was to be feared.

He declared that he would himself pass the first night by the side of his patient. He permitted no one to approach the count, who was still insensible.

Then he unbound the cords. Edmond's long dark locks fell fast beneath the scissors of the doctor's assistant, and compresses of ice were placed upon his burning brow.

CHAPTER X.

HUSBAND AND WIFE.

THUS lay Edmond many days, alternately watched by the doctor and his assistant, till such time as the malady should promise to take a more regular course, and the duty of attending to her husband could be safely intrusted to the countess.

In one of the adjoining rooms she had established herself. She knew that she was not likely to leave it for many weeks; she made her arrangements accordingly. The door between Edmond's chamber and her own she had softly taken out and replaced by *portières* with heavy curtains.

All the windows of her apartment she had masked and covered in the same way.

From the dull red flame in the ground-glass globe of a lamp suspended from the ceiling passed the only light that visited that prison, freely chosen by the solitary inmate of it. If the gloom of external objects can add weight to the dejection of a brain already oppressed by anxious thoughts, heavy indeed must have been the young fair forehead on which that weary lamp-light shone in the long monotonous hours of Juliet's faithful vigil.

But here, in those sleepless watchings by the heavy dreadful curtain, which her hand daily ventured nearer to, and little by little timidly withdrew—here, at

last, from fires long hidden, another light, a light more
ghastly, more lugubrious, entered into her soul, and
lighted up the past, the present, the future, all things,
with its cold funereal glare.

In the livid reflex of that hideous revelation sunk
and ceased forever the humid splendors of those once
soft and spiritual eyes, whose desolate, cold, unswerv-
ing regard had so strangely thrilled me when I first
beheld them years ago.

The light pure blood, whose innocent pulses once
so swiftly moved in every virgin vein of that fair
body, a few broken words sufficed to stagnate forever
in a heart congealed.

A few broken words—an unconscious utterance—
an involuntary confession—dropped by frenzy from
the lips of a maniac!

But those words unveiled the head of Medusa, and
the woman that gazed on the thing they revealed became forthwith a statue.

Such I had seen her.   I shall never forget it.

And so, one morning, when Edmond, awaking re-
freshed from his first peaceful slumber, recovered the
consciousness of his own identity—when, still weak,
but aware, he was able to take notice of the things
around him, and, with a sick man's languid sense of
returning life, he lifted looks of grateful recognition
to the face of his wife watching beside him, that face
was as the face of the Judgment Angel.

"Why didst thou not stretch forth thy hand to
Felix?"

These words were spoken slowly, in a voice almost
inaudible, but they were terribly distinct.

She knew all.

And when he heard those words and saw that face, *he* too knew all.

In the look of deadly inexorable doom which accompanied that searching question, he recognized the reflex of his own soul.

He understood that the traitorous secret, which he had so long immured in his inmost heart, had escaped from a breast no longer guarded, and the voice that now audibly accused him was the voice of his own conscience. .

Before him stood his crime.

Not the rash act of man overborne by passion, in which man's will and mind have no part. Slave of Passion he had never been, but slave of the Thinking Power.

Only in the act of his mind was his crime. A demon thought.

CHAPTER XI.

CAUSE AND EFFECT.

IN the evening of the day when Juliet and Felix first revealed their hearts to each other, they paused on their homeward path by the outskirts of the forest.

Juliet heard a moan in the underwood.

It was Edmond's.

Felix, too, heard something stir in the bushes.

It was Edmond's footstep.

He had been urged back to the chateau by that inexplicable inquietude which precedes the outbreak of passion, like the fume which rises before the flame leaps forth.

What passed within him then, and all that happened immediately afterward, we know.

Accustomed to coop and mew himself up within the strict inclosure of his own mind for single and mortal combat with the new and boisterous power that was then assailing him, he summoned all his pride in aid of a supreme effort to hide, at least, from every eye the desperate struggle from which he could no longer withdraw his spirit.

We also know that in this, unhappily for himself, he succeeded only too well.

It was with this object that he announced his intended alliance with the Rosenberg heiress. For a moment, perhaps, he seriously entertained that intention.

"Yet another year of struggle," he said to himself, "and I shall have mastered this mad passion which has its roots in the error of a whole life."

But ever before his eyes imprudently played and sported the heedless happy pair to whom was given that Paradise from which he was banished. They were indifferent to, because ignorant of, the intense torture that was devouring his heart. There was none to see how he suffered: no gratitude, no tenderness, no pity, for his unguessed pain.

Not one, of those for whom they were endured, divined or recognized the thousand silent sacrifices which daily he imposed upon himself.

He would have undertaken and overcome yet greater difficulties in order to hide these numberless, nameless abnegations from mistrustful or suspicious eyes.

He honestly wished to hide them.

But those from whom he sought to hide them were so lightly, easily cheated; they took so readily for granted the utter absence of all that torment which he was at pains to conceal; they believed him so promptly, so implicitly, that he was exasperated by his own success.

And no ebullition, no escape in word, or look, or act, relieved this intolerable anguish.

From his earliest years he had brought, with mathematic precision, his voice, his manners, even the lines of his face, into a harmony undisturbed by expression.

And this, which had once been natural to him, he was now obliged to continue by imitation as a part to be played. He was constrained to be the actor of his former self.

His whole being, therefore, became to him a mask. Under this mask he was smothering, but he could not take it off.

Too soon in life his sensations and feelings had been forced into those directions upon which Youth joyously turns its back. He had reversed the order which the course of nature assigns to the life of man.

Even as a boy his affections had a sort of paternal character. These fatherly feelings in a child, the sense of superiority which they implied, and the habit of an authority which was almost thrust upon him by the instinctive and spontaneous submission of those about him, were experiences which, however pure they were, and noble in themselves, he attained to the knowledge of too soon.

He had overleaped those stages in a man's life which are perhaps perilous to traverse, but which can not be left out nor avoided with impunity.

That is the "*Sturm und Drang*" period—the season of storms.

The purifying fire of Passion ennobles the ardors of Youth, and only finds in youth the place to which it is native and inborn. In youth Desire can claim by right and title its natural and legitimate satisfaction. It finds its excuse in the coercive force of that necessary law which coincides with liberty: the law of the life of the creature, according to which it is bound to live. Passion, at that period, lightly evaporates in the fume of its own joyous intoxication, and does not deposit at the bottom of the soul the bitter residue of repentance.

Man shares the world with all created things on

equal terms. Those requirements which are universal to his nature and his age, each is authorized to satisfy. And, even in its errors and its heats, Youth pays tribute to the divine government of Nature. Then the life of a man is in the privileged enjoyment of its full rights. Even as, by the nature of it, it is compelled to give, so is it authorized to take. And if, at that time, the breath of error should obscure with its light and fleeting cloud the clear mirror of the soul's purity, remorse at least is without bitterness, and even pain caresses where it wounds. For then the great horizons of life are opened round on every side, wherethrough the spirit bloweth as it listeth; and to the sorrow and the wrong which in after life lie close, staining and rotting where they cling, then the lightest passing wind gives wings, and they are carried away upon the summer cloud, and melted into the summer rain.

It is otherwise with the man who has reversed, in the arrangement of his life, this wholesome order of things, and undertaken to carry loads which, disproportioned to the natural strength of his shoulders, he can only sustain the weight of by ascetic severity of mind. The man who does this, like Angelo,

> "Most ignorant of what he's most assured,
> His glassy essence,"

exaggerates the worth of the life he has lived—mistakes the nature and the value of it, and forgets that *prudence* is not yet *virtue*.

When Edmond buried his youth prematurely under the load of responsibility assumed in taking fatherly

charge of the youth of those two children, Juliet and
Felix, the too-early exercise of an authority, accorded
before it could be claimed, allured his mind into a
fatal conviction of the infallibility of its own judgment.

He contemplated life too coolly, and too partially
because too strictly, since human life, which is merely
a mass of incongruous materials to be wrought and
welded into shape by the violent tact of warring antagonisms, can not be prearranged into symmetrical
system except by ignoring and excluding whatever
will not fit into mathematical form. Edmond under-
rated the difficulties of life so long as his own veins
remained ungoaded by the promptings of the blood,
of which the natural savagery in every man was to
him unknown. And thus the disturbing element,
which he had neglected to take into account, ended
by bursting every barrier, and sweeping all before it.

Then began for him (all the preceding extracts from
his writings prove it) a series of internal conflicts in
which those intellectual weapons, whereon his reliance
was placed, fell shivered one by one against the obtuse
enormous fact of an incomprehensible passion.

Forced to search in ever deeper and remoter recesses of that intellectual arsenal for the sophisms that
supplied him with the means of warfare, he ended
(when pushed to the last extremity) by cowering for
shelter behind the bulwarks of a barren Fatalism.
Nor did he perceive that he had squandered the most
precious materials of his soul in the construction of a
mere dead wall.

By the ring of Amasis, which was already firmly

forged about his destiny, the motive power of his being was cabled to Superstition, that last anchor of the man without Faith. The real or supposed signification of the antique inscription began to flatter and caress the natural tendencies of his mind in proportion as the wholesome development of Desire became more and more obstructed by Circumstance. Hemmed round by perils of which his rising passion forewarned him with menace at every moment, and conscious that to wish is to be weak, he sought, in his dealings with Circumstance, to annihilate temptation by canceling the initiative prerogative of Will.

Thus he resigned the highest and most necessary privilege of a reasonable being in suppressing the exercise of that faculty which is not determined nor controlled by sensuous objects, but which, by virtue of an origin directly divine, subjugates these, and Nature herself, to its own action, and is therefore, in its highest development, as holy liberty, continually tending toward absolute good. This noble activity he forewent, to watch with folded arms the tricksy turn of a blind Chance.

To him, therefore, the world of hopes and fears, in which souls are saved and lost, became a jumbled coil of crazy circumstance. Whatever might be imposed upon him by the Fate that ruled this dizzy planet of his own invention, he was resolved to bear unflinching. But he was equally decided not to repel nor reject the golden gift, whenever that fickle Power might chance to fling into his open hand the thing he dared not purchase at the too great price of a crime, but which he had courage to contemplate in the alluring

N

imagery of a dream, with a passionate longing to possess it.

He was under the dominion of this state of mind when his brother engaged him to join the shooting expedition down the river on that fatal fourteenth day of September.

He went unwillingly, haunted by bad forebodings; and, as if every thing was in conspiracy against him, Felix, on that morning, was in a bantering, aggressive humor.

In proportion as Edmond was unusually sombre and thoughtful, Felix, full of the insolence of unusually high spirits, unconsciously did every thing that the most malignant forethought could have devised to irritate, exasperate, and madden his brother's bitter mood.

At every moment, seeing Edmond so silent and so sad, he would ask him if his thoughts were not with his Rosenberg heiress, his prudently-selected bride? Then, getting astride upon the bulwarks of the boat, and rocking it from side to side with an aggravating silly restlessness, "What fun," said he, "to think of the rage of all the lawyers, when, with the money saved from their clutches, you buy your future countess her precious tiara of diamonds! Anyhow, it will not be as fine as this, my good fellow!" And he flashed the sparkling amethyst in the sun's bright rays. "No; not for all the gold in the world will you match me the worth of this!"

"Beware! beware!"

In Edmond's heart an inward voice was calling.

Felix grew gayer and gayer; Edmond ever colder, more monosyllabic, sullen, taciturn.

In presence of the keeper's boy (as we know), he had warned his brother of his imprudence, and repeatedly besought him to sit still. ' But the lad had left the boat.

They were alone, those two brothers.

Above them, on either side, the high banks, solitary. Beneath them, the deep and rapid stream.

And gliding, gliding, as Life glides neighboring Death, the ever-present chance, through changing sun and shade upon the treacherous surface of that stream, Felix, the happy butterfly, fluttering his careless wings, and Edmond, the brooding melancholy thinker, sullenly strangling in his own breast the moan of a bruised and breaking heart.

"I swear, brother, you are insupportable to-day," says Felix. "But I'll bet you that at least I'll frighten you, if I can't make you merry. Houp là!"

And he began to rock the boat more violently.

Edmond was silent. He sat still and made no answer. But within his inmost being a strange new life began to move. As once before, in the first fierce moment of his great despair, at midnight in the forest by the river-side, he had heard them mutter as they moved, so now again he heard strange voices speaking in the water. And they hissed, and lisped, and laughed from little wicked lips,

> "*Get us the ring! We are here again.*
> *Ho, Brother! Who will be Bridegroom then?*"

An unequal pressure with one foot turned the prow of the boat sharply and suddenly against the current. The boat reeled and dipped to that side. Felix lost his balance, staggered, slipped, fell, disappeared.

Anon he rose to the surface.

His fall had given impulse to the boat. He rose in the wake of it. Striking out with all his strength, he tried to reach it. It was still before him, floating fast upon the rapid stream.

No hand was moved, no oar was stretched from that gliding bark.

Against the whirling water he beat, fast and weak, with desperate arms. His soaked clothes and heavy boots were dragging him down. The light boat glided on.

Suffocating and exhausted, he gasped, "Enough, Edmond! For Heaven's sake, enough! I am sufficiently punished. My strength gives way. I am sinking. I can no more."

Before the eyes of Edmond, in that moment, rose a long-remembered Image. Forms that for many a day and hour had floated in his fancy, following his thoughts, suddenly passed from the inward to the outward world, and in substance palpable appeared before him, clothed with hideous life.

He knew them well, those forms no more of Fancy's making. No new-comers they, but of an ancient date; coeval with the crime of hoary centuries, whose guilty conscience slept not quiet in the grave. He had disinterred them from the depth of ages with the darkness on them; he had released them from their wicked hiding-places in the tombs of Theban kings; he had planted them in the prospect of his eye; he had shrined them in the silent places of his soul—idols of a drear religion, worshiped with the devil worship of despair.

And for many a day and hour they had stood between the seeing of his eye and the displaced shape of wholesome human life, so that looking on them now, he saw *them* only. Not himself, not Felix, the brother of his flesh and blood, but phantoms, ghosts —Sethos the realmless prince, immovable, before Amasis the usurper, sinking to his sudden end. Cold as the spectre of his own thought, erect, unmoved, immovable, with folded arms he stood and looked—

Looked on his drowning brother.

Then into the eyes and over the face of Felix there came an undefinable terror.

It was not the terror of death. It was not the vague alarm of a drowning man.

He had understood the face of his brother Edmond.

He had read in that face the meaning of a thought which sufficed in a second of time to congeal with horror the essence of his soul.

And Felix shuddered.

So the angels must shudder when they gaze into the depths of Hell.

With a voice that was the death-shriek of man's faith in man, he cried, "Edmond! Edmond!"

It was the sad receding message from a world of love submerged.

Side by side, the fleeting river bore them on, those brothers.

The one safe, unmoved, erect.

. The other convulsively struggling with baffled and broken efforts amid the thousand curling, cold, and silvery meshes of that liquid loom of death.

Side by side, the river bore them onward yet. Side

by side, eye fixed on eye, with speechless lips and speaking looks.

A dreadful inutterable dialogue was passing then between the eyes of those two brothers. They understood each other.

And the place, too, was so wickedly silent all this while—so horribly aware. Had it sent but a single human sound from the careless innocent life it was keeping out of sight—nay, not so much! had it bid but a wild bird hoot to stop the deadly duel of those dreadful eyes! But no, it held its peace.

At length, as in an agony of supplication, these last words broke from the lips of the sinking swimmer:

"In the name of the All-merciful God, save *thine* immortal soul! Brother, brother, stretch forth thy hand!"

An arm's length from the boat he sank exhausted. Sinking, his long brown wavy hair spread out—a hideous dusky thing—faint seen an inch beneath the glassy surface. Like a tuft of heaving water-weeds, it rose and fell with the rising and the falling of the rippled waters.

The stretched right arm and imploring hand still rose above the surface.

Involuntarily Edmond leaned forward to seize and grasp it. He had but to stretch forth his hand, and his brother might yet be snatched from destruction.

A heedless sunbeam grazed the glittering jewel upon the right hand of the drowning man, and flashed a violet light into the eyes of Edmond. A voice within his heart called to him,

"*Touch not with earthly finger the work of Fate.*"

He shrank back.

The hand of Felix had disappeared.

Again it rose,

And disappeared again.

Once more, and never more again, it reappeared above the water; not as before—not supplicating now, but rigid, and stiffened by the agony of death; held up to heaven high and stark, and as in menace, not in prayer, for the death-cramp had clasped the fingers and locked the fist. A formidable sight.

It sank and rose no more.

How long sat Edmond with fixed eyes, stupidly staring at the glassy murtherous water, that sleek accomplice of his soul's bad angel?

The distant barking of a dog beyond the banks aroused him.

He started, horror-struck, as from a dreadful dream. He looked around in coldest agony of remorse and terror. He was alone. His dream grinned at him with the leaden eyes of reality.

With a shrill wail he sprang up, and plunged head-foremost into the stream.

CHAPTER XII.

Lex Talionis.

AND Juliet never pardoned Edmond.

Love, perhaps, may survive Esteem, for the cause of love is in itself. It is, and knows not why. But Juliet had not loved Edmond; she had worshiped him. He had committed sacrilege against himself. The God we have knelt to can never kneel to us with impunity. The weakest woman is pitiless to weakness in a man, and the gentlest of a gentle sex has no mitigation of scorn for the man that has betrayed the gentlest quality of her nature—implicit trust.

There is no pardon for desecrated ideals.

CHAPTER XIII.

The Last Tribunal.

I HAD ceased reading. I had ended the perusal of the count's papers. The night was far spent. The hours passed unnoticed. The pages still lay in my hand. The knowledge of their story still weighed heavy on my mind.

Horror and compassion contended within me, disputing in my thoughts the sentence of a human soul, as though it were the Judgment Hour.

"No!" I cried at last.

"No pity for the pitiless! No mercy for the unmerciful!"

When the assassin turns the knife in the breast of his victim in the moment when spume is on the lips, and blood is in the eyes of the dying man, he acts perhaps with pity, willing to bring to speedier end those lingering pangs.

The man who first devised the diabolical machinery of torture, and took fierce pleasure gloating on the shrieks of some tormented wretch, sought thus perhaps to slake the thirst of a burning vengeance, or else he was a savage, born with the natural wildness of an untamed brute, and used to bloody business.

But this man?

By so much the more nobly natured, the more deeply damned; for in him, all large and lofty powers, combined, augmented the greatness of his crime by the sum of his virtues.

Ah! didst thou think to find an error in the calculation of Eternal Justice?

Bungler!

Ah! didst thou dream that good undone was no great evil done? That no misdeed was in thy good deed missed?

Fool!

Fool, to forget that Will can only be annihilated by Will; that good unwilled is evil willed. Triple fool and slave, that didst sell thyself to Time and Chance, yet couldst not win the wages of an hour!

Knewest thou not that a moment is master of a life? for it is but for a moment that the materials of a man catch fire, burn up, and show what he is made of. Nay, life's self is nothing more than so much stuff to feed that moment's fire.

The Recording Angel is no scribe. He does but keep the registers we write ourselves, and the hand that signs the Judgment Record is man's own.

Pardon?

Yes, for another. For any other, yes.

For this man, none.

So I spake in counsel with myself, and ended stern upon the law.

Then a soft hand pressed back my brow, a loving arm was wound about my neck, and a dear and well-known voice said to me in a tone of tender reproach,

"Dear heart, again you have passed a whole night long unsleeping; and yet how often have you said, yourself, that the night is no man's friend!"

"An angel has spoken out," I cried, with a touch of self-accusal, as I pressed my wife to my arms.

No, night is not the friend of man. And the inhumanities which night had whispered began to be silenced in my heart as I watched, enlarging on the pallid pane, the light that comes to all when "He maketh his sun to rise upon the unjust and the just."

"Put the horses to at once," I said to the servant, who was half asleep when he answered my bell.

"Dear, you are going out, and yet the day has hardly risen. Let the sleepers sleep, and take, thyself, the rest thou needest."

"No," I said; "from him I seek, rest has long since fled. But I go to bring it back to him, else I am not worthy to call myself a Physician."

And I went.

How describe to you my meeting with that unhappy man? I was unable to utter a word. But I opened my arms wide, wide, and he fell upon my breast.

So leaned he, and so wept he, long—bitterly, bitterly weeping. A poor broken ruin of a man.

But when the hard and indurated anguish of long years began to melt in showers of hot tears, there burst with a convulsive sob from the long-pent, hopeless yearning of a wretched human heart this single indescribably sorrowful word,

"At last!"

Long in my arms he lay. It was a long much-needed luxury of deep-desired relief. Into the hollow places of his heart trickled the kind refreshment —the blessed dews of human pity, and once again he felt his long-lost brotherhood with man in the deep compassion of a fellow-creature.

At last!

"Yes," I said, "at last, poor spirit! for lasting is no human sorrow; and eternal only, and without limit, is the love of the Great Father of us all, who has a pity for each human pang, a pardon for each penitent soul."

The days that followed this had silent voices. Let mine be silent too. I will not babble the daily diagnosis of that weary spirit's slow successive fadings from the verge of a life long forfeit to the grave, nor of the brightening, beautifying ardors of it toward the sunrise slowly seen in the hope of a life redeemed.

At last it came—the year's last hour and his life's. The year was in its end; the world was in its winter; the night was spent beyond the middle hour. Dark and drear, with gusty footsteps on the slumbrous snow, the Old Year went, the New Year came.

In the night of St. Sylvester, the night that melted in the sunrise of the Year 1842, I sat by the death-bed of Count Edmond R——.

All the secret folds of that nature native to nobility, which, exhausting itself in the life-long struggle with a guilty memory, had tended ever backward and upward to its original beauty (for that man's penitence on earth had been excruciating), one by one unveiled themselves to me in the hour when I received his last confession.

And as the pain which he had long repressed melted in softened words from the lips of the dying man, the force of self-retention which had so obstinately fastened him to life gave way, and the shattered body no longer shut the soul, long since impatient, from the entrance to the other world.

Feebly pulsed the vital stream in the languid left hand that I held in mine. Suddenly the motion of it ceased.

I thought that he was dead.

But he lifted himself, and sat up in his bed. His eyes opened wide and large, fixed with bright fervor in an upward look. He stretched his right hand high in the air, as if he there saw something which he sought to seize. His whole frame worked with a convulsive spasm. And suddenly, with intense voice, he cried,

"In the name of the All-merciful God, save my immortal soul! Brother, brother, stretch forth thy hand!"

I shuddered.

For it was, almost word for word, the last cry of the dead Felix that issued then from the lips of his dying brother.

The hour of rendition and repayment had arrived.

Of repayment?

A divine smile broke like a sunbeam from a happy land over the features of the dying man. With that outstretched right hand he seemed to have seized something, which he passionately pressed to his lips.

And as in rapture he pressed that solemn kiss upon the visioned thing I could not see, a sigh of deep relief passed from his fervent lips.

It was his last.

PRAY, GOOD CHRISTIAN PEOPLE, PEACE TO THE SOUL OF EDMOND COUNT R——.

THE END.

HARPER & BROTHERS'

LIST OF NEW BOOKS.

A HISTORY OF THE INTELLECTUAL DE-VELOPMENT OF EUROPE. By JOHN WILLIAM DRA-PER, Professor of Chemistry and Physiology in the University of New York; Author of a "Treatise on Human Physiology," &c., &c. 8vo, Cloth, $3 50.

MEMOIR OF THE LIFE AND CHARACTER OF THE LATE HON. THEO. FRELINGHUYSEN, LL.D. By TALBOT W. CHAMBERS. With Portrait on Steel. 12mo, Cloth, $1 25.

A POINT OF HONOR. A Novel. 8vo, Paper, 25 cents.

LIFE ON A GEORGIAN PLANTATION. Journal of a Residence on a Georgian Plantation in 1838–1839. By FRANCES ANNE KEMBLE. 12mo, Cloth, $1 25.

THE CAPITAL OF THE TYCOON: A Narrative of a Three Years' Residence in Japan. By Sir Rutherford Alcock, K.C.B., Her Majesty's Envoy Extraordinary and Minister Plenipotentiary in Japan. With Maps and Engravings. 2 vols. 12mo, Cloth.

HARPER'S HAND-BOOK FOR TRAVELLERS IN EUROPE AND THE EAST: being a Guide through France, Belgium, Holland, Germany Austria, Italy, Sicily, Egypt, Syria, Turkey. Greece, Switzerland, Russia, Denmark, Sweden, Spain, and Great Britain and Ireland. By W. Pembroke Fetridge. With a Map embracing Colored Routes of Travel in the above Countries, and a new Railroad Map. Revised and Enlarged Edition. Large 12mo, Cloth, $3 00; Leather Tucks, $3 50.

ELEANOR'S VICTORY. A Novel. By the Author of "Aurora Floyd." (*In Press.*)

JOHN MARCHMONT'S LEGACY. A Novel. By the Author of "Aurora Floyd." (*In Press.*)

LIVE IT DOWN. A Story of the Light Lands. By J. C. Jeaffreson, Author of "Olive Blake's Good Work," "Isabel; the Young Wife and the Old Love," &c. 8vo, Paper. (*Nearly Ready.*)

M'GREGOR'S SYSTEM OF LOGIC. A System of Logic, comprising a Discussion of the various Means of acquiring and retaining Knowledge, and avoiding Error. By P. M'Gregor, A.M. 12mo, Cloth, $1 00; Sheep, $1 25.

MISS MULOCK'S FAIRY STORIES. The Fairy Book. The best Popular Fairy Stories selected and rendered anew. By the Author of "John Halifax, Gentleman," "Olive," "The Ogilvies," &c., &c. Illustrations. 16mo, Cloth, $1 00.

ST. OLAVE'S. A Novel. 8vo, Paper, 50 cents.

A FIRST FRIENDSHIP. A Tale. 8vo, Paper, 25 cents.

KNAPP'S FRENCH READING-BOOK. CHRESTOMATHIE FRANÇAISE; Containing I. Selections from the best French Writers, with Copious References to the Author's French Grammar. II. The Master-Pieces of Molière, Racine, Boileau, and Voltaire; with Explanatory Notes, a Glossary of Idiomatic Phrases, and a Vocabulary. By WILLIAM J. KNAPP, A.M., Professor of Modern Languages and Literature in Madison University, N. Y. 12mo, Cloth. (*Nearly Ready.*)

HOOKER'S NATURAL PHILOSOPHY. Science for the School and Family. Part I. Natural Philosophy. By WORTHINGTON HOOKER, M.D., Professor of the Theory and Practice of Medicine in Yale College, Author of "Child's Book of Nature," "Natural History," "First Book in Chemistry," &c. Illustrated by nearly 300 Engravings. 12mo, Cloth, $1 00.

CHRONICLES OF CARLINGFORD. A Novel. By Mrs. OLIPHANT, Author of "The Life of Edward Irving," "The Last of the Mortimers," "The Days of My Life," "The Laird of Norlaw," "The House on the Moor," &c. 8vo, Paper, 75 cents; Cloth, $1 00.

KINGLAKE'S CRIMEAN WAR. The Invasion of the Crimea: its Origin, and an Account of its Progress down to the Death of Lord Raglan. By ALEXANDER WILLIAM KINGLAKE. With Maps and Plans. 2 vols. 12mo, Cloth. (*Vol. I., Price $1 50, just ready.*)

THE BOYHOOD OF MARTIN LUTHER; or, the Sufferings of the Heroic Little Beggar-Boy, who afterward became the Great German Reformer. By HENRY MAYHEW, Author of "Young Benjamin Franklin," "The Peasant-Boy Philosopher, or the Life of Ferguson the Astronomer;" "The Wonders of Science, or Young Humphrey Davy," &c. With Illustrations. Small 12mo, Cloth gilt. (*In Press.*)

SYLVIA'S LOVERS. A Novel. By Mrs. GASKELL, Author of "Mary Barton," "Cranford," "My Lady Ludlow," "North and South," "The Moorland Cottage," "Right at Last," &c. 8vo, Paper, 50 cents.

A DARK NIGHT'S WORK. A Tale. By Mrs. GASKELL, Author of "Sylvia's Lovers," "Mary Barton," &c. 8vo, Paper, 25 cents.

GENERAL BUTTERFIELD'S CAMP AND OUTPOST DUTY. Camp and Outpost Duty for Infantry. With Standing Orders, Extracts from the Revised Regulations for the Army, Rules for Health, Maxims for Soldiers, and Duties of Officers. By DANIEL BUTTERFIELD, Major-Gen. Vols., U. S. A. *Approved by the War Department.* 18mo, Flexible Cloth, 60 cents.

HARASZTHY'S GRAPE CULTURE AND

WINE-MAKING. Grape Culture and Wine-Making; being the Official Report of the Commissioner appointed to investigate the Agriculture of Europe, with especial Reference to the Products of California. By A. HARASZTHY. Numerous Illustrations. 8vo, Cloth, $5 00.

LOOMIS'S ELEMENTS OF ARITHMETIC. The

Elements of Arithmetic: Designed for Children. By ELIAS LOOMIS, LL.D., Professor of Natural Philosophy and Astronomy in Yale College, and Author of a Course of Mathematics, &c. 16mo, 166 pages, Half Sheep, 30 cents.

BALDWIN'S AFRICAN HUNTING. African

Hunting from Natal to the Zambesi, including Lake Ngami, the Kalahari Desert, &c., from 1852 to 1860. By WILLIAM CHARLES BALDWIN, Esq., F.R.G.S. With Map, Fifty Illustrations by Wolf and Zwecker, and a Portrait of the Great Sportsman. Small 8vo, Cloth, $1 50.

PRINCIPIA LATINA. PART I. A First Latin

Course, comprehending Grammar, Delectus, and Exercise Book, with Vocabularies. By WILLIAM SMITH, LL.D., Author of the "History of Greece," and Editor of a "Classical Dictionary" and the "Dictionary of Greek and Roman Antiquities." Carefully Revised and Improved by Professor HENRY DRISLER, of Columbia College, N. Y. 12mo, Flexible Cloth, 60 cents.

SEA-KINGS AND NAVAL HEROES. A Book

for Boys. By JOHN G. EDGAR, Author of "History for Boys," "Boyhood of Great Men," "Footprints of Famous Men," "Wars of the Roses," &c., &c. Illustrated by C KEENE and E. K. JOHNSON. 16mo, Cloth, 75 cents.

LINES LEFT OUT; or, some of the Histories left Out in "Line upon Line." This First Part relates to Events in the Times of the PATRIARCHS and the JUDGES. By the Author of "Line upon Line," "Reading without Tears," "More about Jesus," "Streaks of Light," &c. Illustrated. 16mo, Cloth, 75 cents.

WILKIE COLLINS'S NO NAME. NO NAME. A Novel. By WILKIE COLLINS, "Author of "The Woman in White," "Queen of Hearts," "Antonina," &c. Illustrated by JOHN McLENAN. 8vo, Cloth, $1 50; Paper, $1 25

BARRINGTON. A Novel. By CHARLES LEVER, Author of "Charles O'Malley," "Gerald Fitzgerald," "The Martins of Cro' Martin," "Maurice Tiernay," "The Dodd Family Abroad," "One of Them," &c., &c. 8vo, Paper, 50 cents.

MISTRESS AND MAID. A HOUSEHOLD STORY. By DINAH MARIA MULOCK, Author of "John Halifax, Gentleman," "A Life for a Life," "Olive," "The Ogilvies," &c., &c. 8vo, Paper, 50 cents.

TROLLOPE'S ORLEY FARM. ORLEY FARM. A Novel. By ANTHONY TROLLOPE, Author of "Framley Parsonage," "Doctor Thorne," "The Bertrams," "Castle Richmond," "The Three Clerks," "The West Indies and the Spanish Main," &c. Illustrated by J. E. MILLAIS. 8vo, Paper, $1 25 ; Cloth, $1 50.

HARPER'S PICTORIAL HISTORY OF THE GREAT REBELLION IN THE UNITED STATES.

The work will be issued in Numbers, as rapidly as is consistent with thorough and careful preparation. The Publishers hope to be able to issue two Numbers each month.

Each Number will contain 24 pages, of the size of *Harper's Weekly*, profusely illustrated, and printed in the best manner, from large and legible type.

The price of each Number, containing matter equivalent to an ordinary volume, will be Twenty-five Cents.

Booksellers, News Dealers, and Canvassing Agents will be supplied on the most liberal terms.

SPRINGS OF ACTION. By Mrs. C. H. B. RICHARDS. 12mo, Cloth, $1 00; Cloth, Gilt Edges, $1 25.

RUSSELL'S AMERICAN DIARY. My Diary North and South. By WILLIAM HOWARD RUSSELL, LL.D. 8vo, Paper, 50 cents; Cloth, 75 cents.

WILLSON'S PRIMARY SPELLER. A simple and progressive Course of Lessons in Spelling, with Reading and Dictation Exercises, and the Elements of Oral and Written Compositions. By MARCIUS WILLSON, Author of the "School and Family Readers." 16mo, Half Bound, 12 cents.

STANDARD WORKS

Harper & Brothers, Franklin Square, N. Y.,

SUITABLE FOR OFFICERS AND MILITARY STUDENTS.

☞ Sent by mail, postage free, on receipt of Price.

THH BIVOUAC AND THE CAMP. The Bivouac and the Battle-field; or, Campaign Sketches in Virginia and Maryland. By GEORGE F. NOYES, Capt. U. S. Volunteers. 12mo, Cloth, $1 25.

CAMP AND OUTPOST DUTY FOR INFANTRY. With Standing Orders, Extracts from the Revised Regulations for the Army, Rules for Health, Maxims for Soldiers, and Duties of Officers. By DANIEL BUTTERFIELD, Major-Gen.Vols., U. S. A. 18mo, Flexible Cloth, 60 cents. *Adopted by the War Department.*

MODERN WAR: ITS THEORY AND PRACTICE. Illustrated from celebrated Campaigns and Battles. With Maps and Diagrams. By EMERIC SZABAD, Captain U. S. A. 12mo, Cloth, $1 25.

GENERAL SCOTTS INFANTRY TACTICS; or, Rules for the Exercise and Manœuvres of the United States Infantry. 3 vols. 24mo, Cloth, $3 00. *Published by Authority of the War Department.*
The Volumes sold separately, at $1 00 each.
Vol. I. *Schools of the Soldier and Company.*
Vol. II. *School of the Battalion, and Instruction for Light Infantry or Rifle.*
Vol. III. *Evolutions of the Line.*

THE INVASION OF THE CRIMEA: its Origin, and an Account of its Progress down to the Death of Lord Raglan. By ALEXANDER WILLIAM KINGLAKE. With Maps and Plans. Vol. I.. 12mo, Cloth, $1 50.

GENERAL MARCY'S HAND-BOOK FOR OVERLAND EXPEDITIONS. The Prairie Traveler. A Hand-Book for Overland Emigrants. With Maps, Illustrations, and Itineraries of the Principal Routes between the Mississippi and the Pacific. By Colonel RANDOLPH B. MARCY, U. S. A. *Published by Authority of the War Department.* Small 12mo, Cloth, $1 00.

LOSSING'S FIELD-BOOK OF THE REVOLUTION. Pictorial Field-Book of the Revolution; or, Illustrations by Pen and Pencil of the History, Biography, Scenery, Relics, and Traditions of the War for Independence. By BENSON J. LOSSING. 2 vols. 8vo, Cloth, $10 00; Sheep extra, $11 25.

CREASY'S FIFTEEN DECISIVE BATTLES. The Fifteen Decisive Battles of the World; from Marathon to Waterloo. By E. S. CREASY, A.M. 12mo, Cloth, $1 25.

ALISON'S MILITARY LIFE OF MARLBOROUGH. Military Life of John, Duke of Marlborough. With Maps. 12mo, Cloth, $1 75.

MOTLEY'S DUTCH REPUBLIC. The Rise of the Dutch Republic. A History. By JOHN LOTHROP MOTLEY. With a Portrait of William of Orange. 3 vols. 8vo, Cloth, $7 50.

MOTLEY'S UNITED NETHERLANDS. History of the United Netherlands: from the Death of William the Silent to the Synod of Dort, With a full View of the English-Dutch Struggle against Spain, and of the Origin and Destruction of the Spanish Armada. By JOHN LOTHROP MOTLEY, LL.D., D.C.L., Author of "The Rise of the Dutch Republic." 2 vols. 8vo, Cloth, $5 00.

CARLYLE'S FREDERICK THE GREAT. Vol. 3.
History of Friedrich II., called Frederick the Great. By
THOMAS CARLYLE. Vol. III., with Portrait and Maps.
12mo, Cloth, $1 50.

VANE'S PENINSULAR WAR. Story of the
Peninsular War. By General CHARLES W. VANE, Marquis
of Londonderry, &c. New Edition, revised, with consider-
able Additions. 12mo, Cloth, $1 00.

CURTIS'S HISTORY OF THE CONSTITUTION.
History of the Origin, Formation, and Adoption of the Con-
stitution of the United States. By GEORGE TICKNOR CUR-
TIS. Complete in two large handsome Octavo Volumes.
Cloth, $5 00.

STORY ON THE CONSTITUTION. A familiar
Exposition of the Constitution of the United States. De-
signed for the use of School Libraries and General Readers.
With an Appendix, containing important Public Documents
illustrative of the Constitution. By Judge STORY. 12mo,
Cloth, $1 00.

CLAIBORNE'S LIFE OF GEN. QUITMAN.
Life and Correspondence of John A. Quitman, Major-Gen.
U. S. A., and Governor of the State of Mississippi. By J.
F. CLAIBORNE. With a Portrait on Steel. 2 vols. 12mo,
Cloth, $3 00.

CARLETON'S BUENA VISTA. The Battle of
Buena Vista, with the Operations of the "Army of Occu-
pation" for one Month. By Captain CARLETON. 12mo,
Cloth, $ 1 00.